C000068018

ACKNOWLEDGEMENTS

Thanks to Kathy Eyles who took my writings and typed them up
To Leslie Ion and Phil Herrick for putting it all together on a disk
and then printing
To Bob Ockenden for reading the very rough copy
To my daughter Janice for her help and encouragement
To Mavis and Sydney Hayes for their help – and Mavis's sketches
To Marcia and Jenny for reading and putting the pages together in
manuscript form
To my newly found friends in Liverpool, England, who encouraged
me to have it published
To Plowright Press who had the courage to produce this book
To the Editor whose enthusiasm made me believe in myself again

Flo baking bread in her kitchen, 1997

CONTENTS   Page

EDITOR'S FOREWORD

In the 1920s Flo Hickson (nee Brown) and her older half-sister Gwynneth were living in Liverpool when they were put into Barnardo's Homes by their stepfather. His son, their younger half-brother Joe, had rickets and was in a children's hospital for more than two years.

Joe's father took him home while Flo became a seven-year-old migrant to Western Australia and Gwynneth stayed in the Barnardo's home in Essex. In the 1990s each of the three thinks she/he had the worst childhood.

Flo's story, therefore, stands as a testimony of children who suffered abuse or privation of any kind, whether they were in an institution or not, and of children who survived those forces which tried to crush their spirit, to keep them in their place.

British migration of children is as old as the first colonies but the emotional tragedy that was the legacy for many of them has been brought into the open only in the last decade.

Their distress did not necessarily go unremarked at the time, of course. For example, more than 50 years ago the regime at the Western Australian farm school where Flo was sent (Kingsley Fairbridge Farm School, Pinjarra) had its its critics. Not least of these were Geoffrey Thomas, who worked there from August 1939 to November 1940, Tempe Woods, after-care officer 1940-43, and Faith Missingham, the teacher at the Domestic Science School at Fairbridge for whom Flo was to work. The reasons for their criticism, and that of London Fairbridge Society, are set out at the end of the book, as part of the historical background to Flo's migration.

i

Various points the critics made I have also put in text footnotes, which expand on what Flo has written. These draw largely, as does the historical background, on documents in the Fairbridge Archive, which is in the Department of Special Collections and Archives at the University of Liverpool. Extensive recataloguing of the Archive coincided with the deadline for getting the book to the printer. This meant that reference numbers could be used only for the main sections, as sub-sections had still to be decided.

Apart from Archive documents and reference numbers noted at the end of the historical background, for reasons of space there is no separate bibliography. However, the first mention of books in the historical background, as well as in text footnotes, is full enough for reference purposes.

Thanks
My thanks to all those individuals and staff who gave so generously their time, effort and interest: Gwynneth and Bill Jones; Joe and Marion Massey; Violet Freeman and Mary Doughty; Di Scott at Fairbridge, London; Simon Wilson, Archivist (Social Work Project), University of Liverpool; Barnardo's, Essex; Battye Library, Perth, Western Australia; Birmingham Central Library; Liverpool Central Library including the Local History Library and Record Office; Windsor Castle, Royal Archives; RAC Western Australia; Kirsten Robinson at Parliament House, Perth, WA; above all, to Flo who has been tremendous to work with and whose life story has brought such insights.

Anne Bott
Warwick, November 1997

1. BEGINNINGS, IN WALES AND LIVERPOOL

My mother's name was Ruth Fielding and she had a sad life. Her first husband, George Brown, was a munitions worker who was killed in an explosion in July 1917, three months before the birth of their daughter Gwynneth Georgina.

My mother met him in Wales where she went to work at a farm. Before that she and her sister were in a Home for girls in Liverpool, their brothers in a Home for boys. Their father was a dock worker.

George Brown had also worked on a farm, at Llanpumsaint, north of Carmarthen. My mother was not far away, at Llandysul. He was twenty nine when he died, blown up in the accident in the nitro glycerine section at HM Pembrey explosives factory.

After Gwynneth was born in October 1917, my mother stayed in Carmarthen until shortly before my birth when her married sister Elizabeth Doughty fetched her back to Wavertree, Liverpool, to be near her family.

My mother got compensation under the Workmen's Compensation Act for her and Gwynneth after George Brown's death and she had to go to the County Court of Lancashire at Liverpool to ask for it to be transferred. Before I was born, on 31 January 1921, it was ordered that she was to be given £15 out of the balance of the money and able to draw four pounds ten shillings (£4 10s; £4.50p) every month.

She had a lock-up shop, a general store, in Wellington Road, Wavertree, and she made toffee apples on Sundays which our cousins came over to eat.

The man I remember as my father used to bounce me on his hand high into the air. I loved this game and chortled with delight. I loved him too, dearly.

Then suddenly he was not there any more. I remember the scream of a whistle, a factory whistle I think, and terror, my mother grabbing me in her arms and running with me. She stood me firmly against a brick wall and told me not to move.

I knew he had died. I was not yet two years of age.

My mother decided to marry Joe Massey, a lamplighter. Now Aunt Lizzie had warned against this. The family knew him, he visited Aunt Lizzie, and they said Joe was all show. Good looking, but a womaniser and a drinker.

After my mother died, Massey married twice more. My brother Joey remembers they flitted from rooms to rooms, the rent unpaid, always one step ahead of the landlord, pushing a handcart hired for 6d (sixpence; 21/2p) to carry their belongings. My stepfather became a qualified upholsterer later, and at one time was in charge of a factory production line, but he still drank. Joey remembers having bare feet and going hungry.

We moved nearer the centre of Liverpool, to Pine Street, and my mother married my stepfather in December 1922. He was all Aunt Lizzie had predicted. My mother was pregnant and there were terrible arguments all the time. She used to roam the streets at night to get away from him and once the police brought her home.

She gave birth to a boy, my brother Joey, and from then I turned my affections to him. His birth made no difference to our stepfather. He carried on as before.

Then we moved to Almond Street, off Upper Parliament Street, to one room at Mrs McCarthy's, number 37. Alfonsus McCarthy was a ship's steward. My mother took in ironing and went out cleaning again to earn enough to feed the family and pay the rent.

Gwynneth did all she could for Mother, helping with housework and shopping, and I kept watch over Joey, playing beside him as he slept in the bottom drawer of Mother's Welsh dresser. I used to sit on the floor and play games with cherry pips, the same games I later played with marbles, rolling them on the floor to hit the main stone.

Our room was not very large. As well as the dresser, it contained in one corner a bed. There were also Mother's dining table and chairs in another corner and the large blue armchair which I used to cuddle up in especially if I was feeling scared or unhappy. But there was not enough space to set up the Welsh crib and she could not use it.

I loved sliding down the banisters to the cellar and spent many delightful hours doing this. Gwynneth fetched the coal from the cellar for the fire in our room. She used to hide in the cellar, it was long and black, whenever there was a bad storm for she believed the lightning would strike the steel frame of her glasses.

I used to tease her and would sing out as I slid down the banisters: "Cowardy, cowardy custard, scared the lightning will hit her glasses and kill her."

One day Mother came home very tired. Gwynneth was asked to cook tea. Mother noticed she needed more milk and asked Gwynneth to go and fetch her purse. "Here you are, Mummy," said Gwynneth as she brought it back. Mother opened her purse, it was empty. It was too much and she started to cry.

"Please don't cry," said my sister, "we will manage." Gwynneth tried to look after Mother. She used to hide Mother's purse, but my stepfather would follow her and find it and take the money for

3

drink. He hit Gwynneth often, as well as my mother, and physical violence was not the only abuse he subjected my sister to.

I was four years old when Mother was pregnant again. Throughout the pregnancy, she was sick and spent most of her time in bed. Aunt Lizzie came by often, bringing our cousins. My mother would cry to Lizzie: "Look what he has brought me to, what will I do?" My cousins, Harry and Jack, looked after Gwynneth, who was found crying after being bullied by lads throwing stones in the street.

All of a sudden the room was empty of people. Aunt Lizzie told me that my mother had gone to hospital to be cared for. I would think now that the cause of her hospitalisation through all the weeks before my brother was born was bad nutrition.

On 11 October 1925 my mother had her baby, a boy called Harold. Harold never came home from hospital and Mother used to visit every day to feed him. I remember the clanging of the tram and I would wait for her to come in.

One day a few weeks later I heard the clanging of the tram bell and listened for my mother. Instead of her usual greeting I heard an argument with my stepfather before she screamed and fell to the floor. There was the sound of activity and then silence. My mother was taken to hospital but did not return this time. Suddenly loneliness and fear descended, my mother had died.

My mother's death certificate, dated 8 December 1925, read: "At 9.45 this evening Ruth Massey died at Brownlow Hill. Cause of death Mitral Regurgitation – Cardiac Failure (No PM) (post-mortem examination)."

My brother's death certificate, also dated 8 December 1925, read: "At 9.55 this evening Harold Massey, two months old, died at Brownlow Hill. Cause of death Unsuitable Feeding – Infantile Asthenia (No PM)."

In 1991 I learnt that my mother and my baby brother Harold were interred in a pauper's grave. I subsequently discovered that this was at Walton cemetery.

It is a continuing source of anguish and distress to me that my mother's death, and my stepfather's attitude, left me without any information about my father, who I truly believe was someone who cared for her and nurtured her after the death of her husband George.

My mother was 32 when she died. This tragedy was to change my life completely.

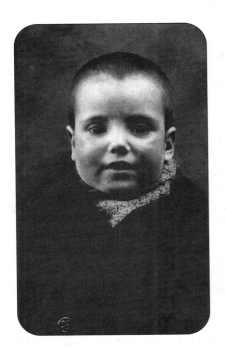 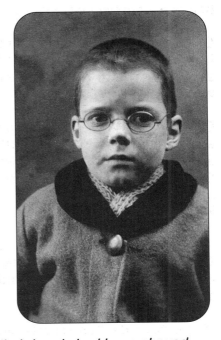

Flo (left) and Gwynneth after their heads had been shaved at Barnardo's in case they had lice. Pictures courtesy of Barnardo's photographic and film archive

2. MAYFLOWER COTTAGE IN BARKINGSIDE

By 12 January 1926 I had become an orphan. My stepfather didn't want us and ignored the offers of Aunt Lizzie to take us into her home. He had one solution only, to put us in the keeping of Barnardo's Homes and refuse to disclose our whereabouts. I would be five years old at the end of that month. Gwynneth was eight years old.

My brother Joey was in Alder Hey, a children's hospital in Liverpool. He was then nearly two and a half years old. He was suffering from rickets and stayed in hospital for over two years before going back to his father. At one time it seemed he was also destined for Barnardo's.

Later I was to find out that my stepfather had been admitted to Barnardo's in July 1913, with a sister and brother, after his mother died in October 1912 from exhaustion following an appendix operation. His father had died from cancer in December 1905.

I don't recall how we actually travelled from Liverpool to the Girls' Village Home at Barkingside, Essex, except one incident. We first went to a place called Stepney (Barnardo's headquarters in the east end of London). It had high thick steps leading up to the building.

I was always to remember this, because later on when I was given bread and dripping, and the bread was cut very thick, it was always referred to as 'Stepney Doorsteps'. We slept that night in a large dormitory, my sister and I slept on one side of the dormitory and were separated from each other by about six beds. This was to prevent us from talking to each other.

Across the other side was a lone boy and I said to my sister: "There's Joey."

"No, it's just a boy off the street," she said.

I would not believe her, for to me it was Joey and the rest of my life was to be dominated by this need to find Joey. I always knew where Gwynneth was but never Joey.

The Girls' Village Home was run by two female Governors. My sister and I were placed in Mayflower Cottage. The cottages were arranged in a large circle surrounding green lawns, part of which we were not allowed to walk on and little notices telling us to keep off the grass warned of this. There were also large shady trees and my sister and I sat beneath them.

Gwynneth and I were put into the same bedroom and this was because being older she had to look after me, to make sure I obeyed the rules and did as I was told. She also took charge of daily tasks of getting up, getting dressed, sewing on buttons, mending my clothes. She said I used to pick at these all the time.

Every night before we went to bed we were given an enamel mug full of scalding milk. I used to love to blow the skin off the top as it formed, it was the greatest joy of my life.

I spent two Christmases at Barnardo's, 1926 and 1927. Father Christmas arrived at our cottage in a horse drawn vehicle. I was the youngest and was sent to greet him at the door. Although I was scared and cried, I still had to do it.

While he left a little sack, I don't recall any gifts. My sister says we could not keep them after Christmas Day. Toys and dolls were kept in a separate room and visitors were taken there and shown all the things, as if we had plenty to play with, but we were not allowed to play with them except on that one day.

We used to go to a very large storeroom for our shoes. When your shoes needed repairing they went to the cobbler's and were soled and heeled again, and then put into the storeroom for another child. I chose long button up boots.

About our meals, I remember one in particular. For midday dinner we were served boiled beef, carrots and cabbage, and the boiled beef was surrounded by a large piece of bright yellow fat. My stomach turned at the sight of it, so I ate everything on my plate (which was compulsory) save that piece of yellow fat. I couldn't think what to do with it.

To eat it was impossible so I dropped it on the floor. I had a nice clean plate but the fat was seen by one of the senior girls. "Who did this thing?" and there was silence. "Who dropped this fat?" she repeated.

The silence continues and I am trembling with fear. The accusations come and back on my plate is the piece of fat, no longer yellow but like me, dead white. I am ordered not to leave the table until every piece is eaten. While I ate every piece, the smell and look of that fat have remained with me and I learnt my first lesson in self control.

On Sundays we went for walks in crocodile formation as it was called, forming into two lines and marching. I loved the smell of the bubbling tar being put on the roads and have loved that smell since.

I often missed out on the Sunday walk, I don't know why I was punished but it seemed it happened to me so regularly. I was either shut in my bedroom for what seemed like hours on end or made to stand in the hall facing the front door. I was not allowed to move around or sit or talk but had to stand waiting until my cottage girls arrived back. The loneliness I felt has never left me and is reflected in this poem I wrote many years later:

What have I done?

You naughty child
You should have stayed in
Not gone outside
In solitude you will remain
A lesson to learn, solitude retain.

What have you done
Why should you know
Peep through the pane
See if there's snow
There is nothing to see
What did you expect
Clear skies with the sun
Shining through Perspex.

Be thankful child
For the things you received
Forget what you've lost
It's not part of our creed.
Love you'll not know
Sorrows your cross
To laugh you were born
Like all the rest
But it's tears you will shed
So mark it well
Lone child it were better
You had been still born.

When we went to church it was packed full with over a thousand girls and the two Governors would take the service. Just before the sermon they would tell us to cough if we needed to, they pronounced it corf. "If you want to corf," they would say, "corf now," and when they gave the instruction everyone coughed.

One of the highlights for me at Barnardo's was presenting the Duke and Duchess of York (who later became George VI and Queen Elizabeth) with flowers during a visit in 1926.

Young Dot Lauder and I were chosen for the job and for weeks before we practised doing a full Court curtsy. I can still do that curtsy. It entails swinging the right leg in a circular movement while sinking completely on to the leg, with downcast eyes and bowed head. My left leg is before me, then Royalty holds out a hand for me to gently touch, to ease myself back into the upright position, still with head bowed.

I used to suffer from psoriasis and because I was nervous my skin broke out, so I was covered all over with a brown ointment (I loved the coal tar smell of this ointment and can still smell it) and then was carefully attired in a snow white singlet and pants, petticoats and a beautiful white dress with a large pink sash. Dot and I carried the basket of flowers between us and presented it to the Duchess.

I have always thought she would never have known how smeared I was beneath the finery. Of course these lovely clothes were handed back for the next occasion and I often wondered whether my outfit was stained beyond further use.

I remember Gwynneth and I had some Easter egg each. We were enjoying it when one of my baby teeth fell out all covered in chocolate. After I showed it to my sister, she told me I would lose all my teeth if I ate any more egg. I cried at this thought and gave her the rest.

Mayflower Cottage was a two storey house. Our bedrooms were upstairs and I can remember as I lay on my bed being able to stare out of the window and see the trams going by in the distance. On foggy nights, I loved seeing the coloured lights of the trams travelling through the mist.

I also felt frightened at the same time and the nursery rhyme, 'Hark Hark, the dogs do bark, the beggars are coming to town', would travel through my mind. This fear would make me slide deep into the bed and, covering my head with the bedclothes, I would find healing in sleep. I was always able to sleep.

There was a high brick wall all around the Village Home and large iron gates in the wall. These gates always seemed to be shut and I was told that the wall was covered in broken bottles to stop us escaping. I don't know if anybody tried to run away, I was too young to contemplate it and too scared of those beggars catching me and carrying me off.

The marriage certificate of Ruth Brown and Joe Massey, giving Ruth's father's surname as Phelan. Flo was told by cousin Bill Phelan that family members initially anglicised their name to Fielding when they left Ireland so that they could get work at Liverpool docks. Another point of interest is Ruth's age. She was born 20 September 1893, so would have been 29, not 28

3. JOURNEY TO AUSTRALIA

I had been at Mayflower Cottage for two years and was seven years of age when I was one of dozens of girls picked to go to Australia in 1928. We were told that Australia was so hot that we would go on horseback to school and in winter it was so wet we would go by rowing boat.

I don't know whether they really believed this or that their knowledge of Australia was so bad. I think they were trying to make the long six week trip to Australia an exciting adventure. I was unable to conceive how far away Australia was and certainly did not understand that I could not return to be with my sister. Silence would fall on all my questions.

There were weeks of hustle and bustle or so it seemed, we had medical examinations of all sorts, eyes, nose, throat, chest, limbs and finally a mental test. We were told we had to be one hundred per cent fit to go to Australia.[1] We were outfitted with shoes and clothes.

Finally the day arrived when I was to leave England forever. We were lined up in rows all dressed as Guides or Brownies and were given a round tin badge stamped with a picture of an emu and a kangaroo. This was our great gift for going to Australia.

We could not hug or farewell those we were leaving behind. I was a tight bundle of misery hugging to myself the only thing I had left,

---

[1] Australia's requirement for A1 migrants became a matter of dispute with the Fairbridge London Society whose policy, it told the Perth Society Chairman in a letter (2 April 1937), was to choose those children who would get the most benefit from a Fairbridge training once poverty and neglect were behind them, not necessarily the apparently best available.

my doll. Later my sister was to tell me they had been threatened with a thrashing should they cry, and in church the following Sunday they sang, 'For those in peril on the sea'. I was too numb to realise that I was also leaving my sister forever. My great pain was still the loss of my dad and my brother.

I hadn't been happy at Barnardo's and believed my sister responsible, probably because she was in charge of me, and now this scary moment of going with all these stern officials, unsmiling, still giving us orders, but no love and affection or comforting words.

We were put aboard our charabanc (coach) to travel to where our ship lay at anchor, the ship's name was SS Ballarat. It was as we boarded the ship that someone took my doll away. It was made of celluloid and I was told I could not take it to Australia as it would burst into flames and start a bushfire. I cried, I had nothing left.

Apparently I cried for five days, so my Guide Lieutenant told me in a letter years later, and if I had cried for one more day they were going to put me off the ship and send me back. Instead we hit a storm in the Bay of Biscay and I nearly died.

There were five girls in my cabin, Jeannie Lucas and I had to share a top bunk, while the other girls had a bed to themselves. Jeannie and I were first given a bottom bunk, but we kept bouncing up and down the top bunk with our feet till the poor girl could take it no longer and we were shifted up top.

I remember part of the storm for whoever was responsible had forgotten to close our porthole and a large wave swept into our cabin, flooding our cases. My case contained a blue paper outfit representing a harebell which I was to wear at the fancy dress ball, all my clothes or so it seemed were stained blue.

We used to dine in what was known to me as the State Room. All of the kids together, whether there were other passengers I can't say, but there must have been for we were given strict instructions on what to do should we feel sick at the dining table. The stewards were all extra kind to us and I being one of the youngest and the smallest of the party received great kindness. One steward we all loved, he was ginger haired and used to fuss over us and make sure we ate well.

This morning at breakfast, I felt sick and told him. I was rushed out by our Staff with a huge cloth pressed against my mouth to prevent me being sick in public.

I was taken away and apparently went into a coma for three days. I can recall coming to and being fed dry biscuits and water, the biscuits being dunked into the water so I could manage to eat them. It was my Guide Lieutenant who wrote and told me months later, saying what a scare I had given them all. They thought they had lost me but it was not to be and I continued on my way to Australia.

We filled in the long weeks by making dish cloths which were to be sent back to Barnardo's. We sat on the deck in a big square with thick cotton thread using wooden needles and knitting what was called Bunny Rabbit stitch, wrapping the wool round the needle twice before knitting which then dropped the stitch in a big loop so that the dish cloth was open weave, not closed.

We also sang together and there were many dialects rending the air. Lots of the songs were crude cockney songs and I have never forgotten them (woe betide us at Fairbridge if we were ever heard singing aloud those words).

I was told by my Cousin Violet that Aunt Lizzie, her mother, had tried hard to find out where we had been sent, but my stepfather had told her that we had gone to Canada with relatives and would never be found.

14

4. ARRIVAL AT FREMANTLE AND PINJARRA

On 28 May 1928 we arrived at Fremantle, Western Australia, the first stage of my new life at the Kingsley Fairbridge Farm School at Pinjarra.[2] I was to be under the control of Fairbridge for the next fourteen years, I was its ward until I was twenty one.

I don't remember the unpacking of us from the ship and finally on to the train which was very slow and uncomfortable. We grumbled about how different these trains were to the ones in England, we asked: "Where are the express trains?" and were told we were on one.

We had been met in Fremantle by Colonel Heath (ex Grenadier Guards), the Principal of Fairbridge, who had lost an arm in war. He was a big man and quite able to control us all.

I remember he promised to give a penny (1 cent; less than 1/2p) to the first person to see a black boy. We were all looking for the two legged variety, but he was teasing us knowing his penny was safe, none of us knew then as he kept singing out: "Look there's one, and another." A black boy was a large bush/grass plant termed the blackboy.

After many hours we arrived at Pinjarra and were put into large buses to travel the few miles along a corrugated gravel road north eastwards to the farm school. It must have been close to dinner time, midday, for a special meal had been prepared. After alighting from the bus, we were lined up and then from a prepared list

[2] Flo was in the 15th party of children sent to Pinjarra, 58 boys and 57 girls, according to a register compiled by W G Mein, Principal from 11 May 1948 to 1 December 1950. London Society minutes (17 May 1928) record that 102 of the 115 children were from Barnardo's.

15

placed into groups, which represented the cottages we were to live in. Jeannie and I, the youngest of the group, were still together.

We were marched into the Dining Hall, a large wooden building, and sat on forms at long trestle tables. I shall never forget that first meal, pea soup and spotted dick. The soup was so thick the spoon stood up right in its centre without falling over, pea soup I would hate forever. Spotted dick I always loved, a big white roly poly pudding filled with currants and rolled up, put into a calico cloth and boiled, and served with custard.

Once the meal was finished, we were marched to the cottages. Jeannie and I held hands tightly together, we were both scared. Colonel Heath was with us trying to lift our spirits and joking about the naming of new cottages.

He read from a long list of names of British great men, battles and places, finally we called out Kitchener Cottage. "And what about the cottage next door?" asked Colonel Heath and added: "You can't have a kitchen without a cook," and so next door became Cook Cottage.

Then fate stepped in, there was an elderly woman, a scary old woman to Jeannie and I, with her worn features, grey hair and gnarled hands. We clung together in real fright and said: "She's the witch from Hansel and Gretel."

We scurried past her to the next cottage for she was sweetly smiling at us and calling us over to her, she wanted to talk to us, but we hid in the crowd of children, too frightened to stop. This woman had other thoughts (though I did not know this for many years to come). She had seen in me the child she never had, a very tiny seven year old with a peaches and cream complexion.

She was to tell me I was a piece of apple blossom the fairies had kissed and had fallen to earth.

5. SHAKESPEARE HOME

She went to Colonel Heath and asked for me to be placed in her cottage, Shakespeare Cottage. He allowed this only if Jeannie Lucas (from whom they could not separate me) came too.

My Cottage Mother's name was Miss Katharine Kittell and though Authority had wanted us to call our Cottage Mothers by the title 'Mother', it was something none of us could do, she was always called 'Miss'. She was to tell me how her years in Australia had been spent as a Governess to wealthy Western Australian families and she was to take me to meet them. She wanted to turn me into a 'lady' and I was to be trained to live like them.

Her behaviour to me varied from nearly smothering maternal love to harsh cruel discipline to stop me developing a 'swollen head' or becoming 'too big for my boots', though as I was to read later it was continually written in my reports that none of this was happening. I was always in fear of punishment but she would not let anyone else severely chastise me.

On arrival at Fairbridge all the clothes issued by Barnardo's in England were taken from us and put in a storeroom, including our shoes. I was not to wear shoes again until I was fourteen years of age and outfitted to go 'out to work'.

Apparently it was considered too costly to keep us all in shoes.[3] I understood from conversations around me there were getting on for four hundred children at Fairbridge at that time. The numbers

---

[3] Ruby Fairbridge said (Fairbridge Farm; Perth, WA, 1948, p. 99) that at the original farm school at Pinjarra footwear was not worn because the area was wet. The children thereby escaped wet feet as well as attendant colds and flu.

varied through the years. Somebody had to pay for our keep and we were told that the English society paid so much per child till we were fourteen and the balance of monies had to be found in Australia. I remember being told this was fourteen pence per head.[4] (The Child Emigration Society at that time had a lot to do with all of this.)

Jeannie and I clung to each other for comfort for many years as we settled into the two storey cottage that was to be our home.

As you walked through the front door, there was a large sitting room built of jarrah, the walls were unlined and let in draughts of cold air. Later, because our Cottage Mother could not stand the draughts, we lined the walls with pictures from English magazines using a paste of flour and water with salt added as a preservative.

Two of those pictures remain with me even now, one of a young girl looking at her mother and saying: "Mummy, don't forget my sinking feeling." It was an advertisement for Oxo. The other was an ad for meat or meat extract, with a drawing of a calf with writing underneath, 'A little bull goes a long way'.

Along the walls were large lockers that held our clothes and acted as seats. The locker lids lifted up and you had to be quick not to catch your finger when dropping the lid. There was a large wooden table in the centre of the room and if I was to sit at it again, it would remind me of all the harsh treatment that orphaned children received.

The writing of letters to my sister, first the copy I had to make, the

---

[4] The Western Australian and Australian Governments and the UK Oversea Settlement Department each agreed in 1922/3 to pay up to 5s a week maintenance for each child, but with provisos such as there being a ceiling on contributions. Top-up revenue from the London Society was obviously needed, eg in 1939 the weekly cost for each child averaged 24s 5d over 11 months, according to a letter (23 January 1940) from Perth Secretary A F Stowe to London Secretary Gordon Green.

sarcastic chastisement over spelling mistakes, the hitting of my knuckles with the ruler for my scribbling (as it was thought by Authority). Instead of the joy of writing a letter every two months or so, the purgatory of being forced. After all the mistakes were corrected, it had to be written in perfect copybook writing with pen and ink, not a blot allowed, until it was passed fit to be mailed to England, censored to make sure I never told my sister how unhappy I was.

The hours spent sitting at that table while by hand I made white pillowslips and petticoats, all French seams so the raw edges were enclosed, for the annual Royal Perth Show (an agricultural show at which craft work was also exhibited).

I was lucky if I stitched more than an inch in the hour because every stitch had to be perfect in size and distance from the previous stitch. You tried never to have to unpick because the work did not look clean and was never to be washed before being put into the show because of competition rules. We had to wear a clean white pinny and had our hands inspected before the agony of the sewing commenced, every few stitches were presented for inspection.

In the left hand corner of the room, there was a large open brick fireplace. The Cottage Mother's chair was placed centrally in front of the fire and we children would squat any old way on the floor and laugh and talk until sent to bed. I remember being teased about my father. I said: "He's a Welshman and I'm Welsh too."

"Speak Welsh then," the voices shouted. Of course I couldn't speak Welsh, but neither could they so I gabbled off meaningless sounds. "That's not Welsh," they cried. I retorted: "You all speak it then." I was never challenged again. I can recall this fireplace with joy, there was the normality of children around that fire.

Another happy memory of the fire was the large enamel jug of hot cocoa sitting on the hob. It was not always there for it was a treat to be savoured, usually on wet cold days following a paper chase. When we arrived back, we quickly changed into dry clothes and then sitting in front of the fire drank our cocoa.

Filling up part of one wall (next to the door of our Cottage Mother's bedroom) was a large bookcase, although I cannot recall the design. Next to the front door was a window and in front of this a treadle sewing machine, which I learnt to use not happily, in trouble all the time till I mastered the treadle. My Cottage Mother often called me over to thread the needle for her and she taught me a trick of placing a piece of white material under the needle, to reflect the light and show up the eye more clearly.

To the right of the sitting room was the kitchen. The laundry was off a passageway from the back door and consisted of two rough stone troughs, a copper (boiler) for heating bathwater, not for laundry work, that went to the communal laundry, and hooks on the wall to hang our coats on returning from school. We all knew our own peg and woe betide anybody who used the wrong peg.

The bathroom led off the laundry and the staircase and playroom. There was a door off the playroom into the Cottage Mother's bedroom and sitting room. The playroom had another long table down the middle and forms each side. There was also a little curtained alcove that contained a tin trunk. The dormitory took up the whole of the top floor and was a long large room that slept seventeen girls, roughly six beds each side, three down the centre and two in the bottom corner, because the dormitory contained a room for the relieving Cottage Mother and the corresponding square held these two beds.

If either of these beds squeaked, Miss Kittell would hear them in her bedroom and she would come upstairs annoyed at the girl who was wriggling. The next day out would come the oil can in an effort to find the squeak.

I remember a funny episode with the beds, the squeaking started, followed by the banging of the stick on the dormitory floor but the squeaking went on. Then the yells of anger, but the squeaking went on and finally came the Cottage Mother, threatening all sorts of punishment. We all wriggled our beds to see if we could produce a squeak.

We finally tracked down the culprit. Off the dormitory was a balcony with a place for an upstairs toilet in later years, in that space was a mother cat who had just given birth to six kittens, all squeaking. We loved it, the cat was allowed to stay there that night but that night only.

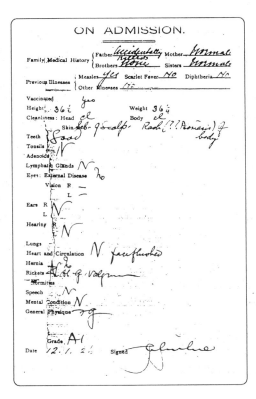

The result of Flo's health check on admission to Barnardo's

6. DAILY ROUTINE

Our daily routine never altered, it was as if we were in the Army for we answered to a bugle call. The bugle wakened me at 5.30 am and I learnt to sing inwardly, 'Get out of bed you sleepy head, get out of bed'.

We were told if we were lying in bed awake the devil found work for idle hands (in this instance, they meant masturbation). The adults had thoughts I never understood, and I was supposed to go to sleep with my hands crossed across my chest.

Sometimes the bedclothes were suddenly pulled back to see if I was doing as I was told. Miss Kittell crept up so silently. She wore crepe soles and they made no noise, although they sometimes squeaked on the polished floor.

On awakening, we would half asleep climb out of bed, kneel down and say prayers:

Now I wake and see the light
God has kept me through the night
Make me good oh Lord I pray
Keep and guard me through the day.

It was all gabbled quickly with no meaning, then I would pull back my bedclothes, stripping the bed it was called. This was to make sure I really made it, then removing the top half of my pyjamas, gather at the top of the stairs.

This routine was the same winter or summer and was very demeaning for the older girls who were developing or already

22

developed. I remember one of our girls had very large heavy breasts and she was unmercifully taunted not only by the girls but the adults as well. (The sense of injustice sank into me.)

The youngest girls first in line, we would run to one of the troughs in the laundry, turn on the cold tap, wash our faces and necks with soap and cold water (cleanliness being next to Godliness) and then splash cold water over our faces, necks and chests to remove the soap. We would run into the bathroom, grab our towels and briskly dry ourselves. These hard harsh towels were supposed to stimulate our skin as we pulled them back and forth across our backs.

Shivering, we would run into the playroom and get dressed, our clothes having been laid out the night before. The soap we used on our skin was Carbolic soap, harsh and full of caustic soda.

My Cottage Mother told me never to use it on my face and taught me to rub my face with the skin of a cucumber as an astringent and occasionally she let me use her witch hazel. She said my skin was too fair and I was not to spoil it. For our hair, we had tins of soft soap, the same as the Carbolic but in soft form.

At the bottom of the stairs was a large chamber pot, placed there for our use during the night, for the toilet was outside, around the back of the cottage. The chamber was to be used by seventeen girls and quite often one would stumble down the stairs, half awake and really no clear recollection. Therefore quite often in the morning this pot would be overflowing.

There we were standing half naked on the stairs and Miss Kittell had seen the overflowing pot. The awful questioning that went on while we stood shivering on the stairs: "Who used the chamber last?" There is no answer. "Own up or you will stand there till you do." Silence. There is shuffling and mumbling as much out of fear as anything and then the accusing of one poor soul.

23

Someone had to take the blame whether she was responsible or not, that person had to take the overflowing pot somehow outside to the toilet, and with a feeling of relief we carried on with our ablutions. Incidents like this were to create in me a deep repressed anger.

I developed such a hate against injustice and was full of frustration because there was no way I could speak out against it and no Authority to go to and discuss my problem. Though there were seventeen girls going through this procedure at the one time, I was never really aware of what anyone else was doing or thinking.

I was very alone and became isolated inside myself, living two lives, one the shut away me, and the other me who obeyed all the rules and tried to please, and was written about in the half yearly and yearly reports, prepared by the school teacher, the Cottage Mother and the Principal.

Once dressed, my next job was to run back upstairs into the dormitory and make my bed. The mattress had to be turned daily. It was made from horsehair, very hard, very thin and quite often the end would be opened, the stuffing pulled out and teased as well as possible, before being pushed back in again and the top resewed.

For the next few nights, my mattress would be good and lumpy before I wriggled it back into shape again. It was inspected by the girl on dormitory duty. I'm sent back downstairs to have my hair done by the older girls whose job it was. Sometimes the girl on duty would pull terribly hard at my hair, really hurting.

I made up my mind that if I ever got that job in later years, I would be quite gentle, and I did end up doing this job when at one stage I had eleven girls under eleven whose hair I had to do each morning before breakfast. Toilet completed it was now work time. (Of course, if you were on hair duty that was your job.)

24

My job for a long time was the dusting and polishing of all the chairs. It was expressed to me that I was so small I did not have far to bend. I hated this job small as I was, I still had to bend and you were never allowed the comfort of sitting on the floor or kneeling.

Other jobs included sweeping, dusting every room or scrubbing benches, table and floor if you were on kitchen duty. We all did our work in silence, quietly and efficiently. That didn't mean that under our breath we didn't sing some of the cockney songs we knew or say sly little phrases to ourselves about the work, the art was to do all these things but not get caught. You kept yourself busy until once again the bugle gave its call.

Lined up in the laundry clean again, our Cottage Mother, when satisfied we were all there and ready, sent us to the Dining Hall. The Dining Hall seemed a long way away, in reality it wasn't, but long enough for me to really suffer on those very cold frosty mornings for, as I have said, we didn't wear shoes.

I would run as fast as I could from the cottage to the Dining Hall over stones all the way, this hurt my feet until they toughened up, but I never got used to the cold or the frost.

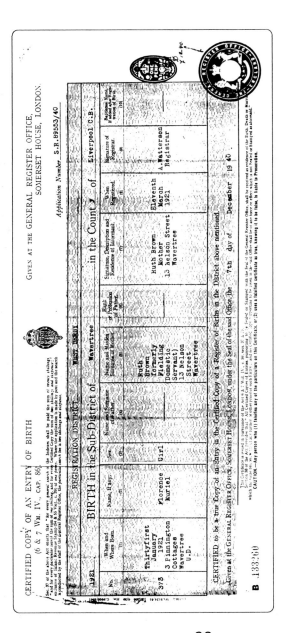

A copy of Flo's birth certificate

Once in the Dining Hall, to my table and sitting on the form, my back to the table, I would let my feet hang, and then the painful burning sensation until my blood pumped warmth back into my feet, oh the joy as the pain left.

We didn't talk and sat as we were until Colonel Heath arrived, always with his megaphone, which he would raise to his lips and address us all as we came to our feet and faced him. "Good morning," he said. "Good morning, Sir," we replied.

The day's announcements were given, the daily running of the place. It could be visits to the Dentist, those going and when; naming those cottages having physical training that evening or dancing lessons, all held in the Dining Hall; ground cleaning; swimming lessons in the river; the Royal Perth Show, who was doing what; any Royal or important visitors; picture show, what nights; any concert we were putting on at or outside Fairbridge.

Finally what I always dreaded, any punishment for so called crimes which included defying their Cottage Mother, forgetting to carry out their communal job, stealing fruit from the orchard. This was done publicly in the Dining Hall, a thrashing with a very flexible cane. I do not recall any girl being publicly punished. Sometimes ten cuts on the hand, sometimes across the backside after being made to bend across the form. We were always told why the person was being punished and we were also told that this was their reward. The punishment never did fit the crimes.

Over the years, two announcements stand out in my memory. Firstly, when the depression hit in the 1930s, we were told we

27

were not allowed to waste a crumb of bread, all food had to be eaten and none dropped on the ground. Any child found wasting food would be punished.

We were also continually reminded that we were British children and not to deprive any Australians of what rightly belonged to them, to the end that we were not to take Australians' jobs. We therefore would be trained for work that Australians didn't want, the boys for farm work and the girls in sewing, baking and housework, to become good farmers' wives. This happened irrespective of the desire or natural ability of the child.

Announcements over, grace was said. "For what we are about to receive may the Lord make us truly thankful. Amen."

Nearly four hundred children sat down, with each Cottage Mother at the head of her table, she did not eat with us but had her meal in the Staff Dining Room. Breakfast was mainly porridge, lumpy and often burnt with plenty of milk. I never remember milk being in short supply. Porridge was followed by bread and dripping or bread and jam. Once breakfast was over it was off to school.

The Staff Dining Room (which I never saw inside until I was about eighteen years old and working at Fairbridge) was sort of halfway between the main Dining Hall and the school. Boys and girls aged fourteen to fifteen who were training to go 'out to work' would have been on duty.

We had some songs we sang about the Cottage Mothers and always knew it was safe to do so when they were eating. We always believed they had better meals than us children.

There is a Dining Hall not far away,
Where all the Matrons sit three times a day,
Oh you should see their eyes when they see the pudding rise,
Oh you should hear their cries: "I want some more."

28

This was sung to one of the old Sankey hymn tunes, 'There is a happy land not far away'.

Looking back at the Dining Hall meals, they always seemed greasy and my stomach would often churn as I forced them down. Whatever was put in front of us had to be eaten. The food was actually wholesome, the cooking spoilt it all. The spinach was overcooked and tasted like sand, potatoes couldn't be spoilt unless they burnt on to the bottom of the saucepan. Cabbage was boiled into a soggy mess and barley soup was made with stock from boiled mutton with all the greasy fat still in it.

The soup smelled of fat and was so thick the spoon used to stand up in it, like it did with the pea soup. I found barley soup one of the hardest meals to eat and remember sitting for what seemed like hours over it. My Cottage Mother told me that if I didn't eat the barley soup, I couldn't have any barley sugar (when we were lucky enough to have this luxury). The fear of punishment was greater than the feeling of revulsion and I dared not be sick.

Desserts we always enjoyed were tarts, steamed puddings – especially spotted dick – and thick custard. Sago was always stodgy and served with treacle folded through and it was cooked in water, not milk.

Once someone gave us a tin of honey. We were sitting on the back steps of our cottage and a large kitchen serving spoon was dipped into the honey and I was told to taste it. It was lovely but, by the time I had finished gorging myself, I felt so sick I was never able to look at or smell honey for years after.

Sometimes apples and oranges were given to us but I remember mostly the grapes. I overate this delicious fruit and my intestines rolled and grumbled and I doubled up with pain, and again it was many years before I enjoyed grapes again.

8. SCHOOL

The school was staffed by State School teachers. They were our only contact outside of Fairbridge. It was an isolated community shut off from the world because, unlike private boarding schools, there were no parents or friends to return to at holiday times. Everybody we knew represented Authority, there was no friendly person to turn to, to cry to, to tell your misery to or be given love and advice in return.

When we arrived at school, it was like being let out of a cage. Freedom to talk, to yell, to run, to skip, to be free and to play all those childhood games of hopscotch, skipping rope and running.

The whistle would blow and we would line up for assembly to be given any notices and then march off to classes. When I left England I was in Standard 1, which was normal for my age. We still had not learnt to write but only to print. In Australia children had to be able to write in Standard 1.

Despite the trauma and being made to feel inadequate, you kept on striving, to receive praise and avoid punishment.

As we children had come from all over Britain, some of the dialects were hard to understand. Teachers became confused when asking simple questions such as: "How many spelling mistakes?" and the answers would come: "Won, Sir," "Non, Sir," "Nun, Sir," "Wun, Sir." By the time the accent had been sorted out and the true answer analysed, their patience was wearing thin and they decided we should all say: "Nil wrong, Sir" if that was the case.

They also decided that every morning at assembly we should

receive speech training. I thoroughly enjoyed it, saying 'a', 'e', 'i', 'o', 'u' and words like dew (= due). In later years I was asked if I taught elocution.

In my second year at school, my report (I got to see my file only in the early 1990s) indicates I repeated the class. I wasn't mastering the writing, but the puzzle for the adults was my height. They could not reconcile my size with my age and were continually thinking my birth must have been recorded incorrectly.

We were not told how we were progressing subject by subject, it was all on our conduct at school, at home. The Sister would add a bit about our health and the Colonel would sum it all up and add his bit after a talk with us in his house.

I was aware I could not spell and was to remain like this until I was nearly twelve when a relieving teacher for the Headmaster's class arrived. He asked of the class: "Who got twenty wrong? Nineteen?" and so on. Somehow he did not make you feel so bad as you stood up and he also considered spelling mistakes a problem that could be overcome.

He started to give words sense and meaning. For the word 'permanent', he said: "Break it up, perm-an-ent." Once he did this, I realised I had been unable to spell because words had never been properly pronounced. I was spelling what I was hearing, not what I was seeing.

I remember the relieving teacher also teaching me to spell the word 'picturesque'. "Picture is easy," he said, "then remember the last part is a trick. Say to yourself, pic-ture-skew, but remember how the skew is spelled, 'sque'."

I never got that word wrong again and I bless that man, for he encouraged me to learn. In a matter of weeks I shot from nil right to nil wrong and my self esteem improved.

Mental arithmetic was no bother. If we were doing a mental test I would breeze through it and was rarely wrong. Similarly, I had little trouble with multiplication, long division, subtractions and square roots, but sit me down with a pad and paper to do problems and, instead of working it out, I would ask myself why I had to do it at all.

One example was an acre (0.4 hectare) of land: if it rained for so long how much rain fell on that acre? All I would see was the acre of land while I pictured 2 inches (51 millimetres) of rain sitting on top of the ground. Another example was how long it took a train to travel a certain distance. My mind saw that slow train travelling fast instead, at 70 miles (113 kilometres) an hour, and I never solved the problem.

Subjects to do with literature I loved. I loved poetry and would test my learning skills with it. I would pick out a poem and as I left school to go to the Dining Hall for midday dinner I would start learning it. It would be say five verses of eight lines per verse.

As soon as dinner finished, I would continue with my learning and by the time the school bell went for the afternoon session I would know the poem off by heart. Sometimes the teacher tested me and i would stand up on the stage and recite. I was not showing off by this, I just loved the words so much. There was one poem I learnt that talked about words:

Words are such lovely things
They jump about and shout with glee
and some have . . .
and some have golden wings like a bee.

The poems I did remember were usually ones that told my story, I know these are not strictly accurate but the words had such an impression on my life. I was actually saying to Authority what I dare not say normally, like the Village School Master (Goldsmith's

The Deserted Village) and the parts:
And still they laughed with counterfeited glee
At all his jokes for many a joke had he . . .
And still they gazed and still their wonder grew
How one small head could carry all he knew.

And Rudyard Kipling's:
If you can keep your head when all about you
Are losing theirs and putting the blame on you . . .
And what is more you'll be a man my friend.

Or Rupert Brooke's:
If I should die think only this of me
That there is some corner of a foreign field
That is forever England.

Or Tennyson's The Babbling Brook:
For men may come and men may go
But I go on forever.

Or in the following poem, I was saying in my childish way we will
rise up:
Where are the snowdrops? said the sun
Dead, said the Frost, buried and lost every one
A foolish answer, said the sun, they did not die
Asleep they lie, every one,
And I will wake them, I the sun,
Into the light all clothed in white, every one.

And Scott's:
Breathes there a man with soul so dead
Who never to himself has said
This is my own, my native land
Whose heart has ne'er within him burned
As home his footsteps he has turned
From wandering on a foreign strand.

England was my home however much they tried to take it away.

As part of literature, I would often be singled out to give an impromptu talk, the subject mostly being chosen by the Headmaster. One day, I was twelve or thirteen years old and in the Headmaster's class, I was askéd to speak on the subject of soap.

Solemnly I stood on the platform and gave a technical account of the making and use of soap. I was rather proud of myself and it probably showed. I had spoken for ten minutes without wondering what to say next. When I had finished and was expecting a word of praise, the Headmaster completely deflated me. He said he was disappointed and thought I could have treated the subject with humour.

I was bothered by this and wondered why he didn't ask me to give a humorous talk. We normally would have been in trouble for doing so, punished for being frivolous and made to write a hundred lines. It was so difficult to be your natural self as you never knew how it would be interpreted. I had to be careful no one in Authority thought I was 'showing off'.

Some of the teachers were genuinely trying to get us to act naturally and trying to bring us out of ourselves, but as we never talked to them as people (only teachers) the communication barrier could not be overcome.

I loved written composition and words flowed out of me, so much so that my writing was always called scribble and I lost marks. When I wrote quickly with pen and ink, the nibs on the pen often needed replacing and because of my heavy pressing the nib would split apart and spatter ink all over the paper. We were forbidden to use pencils.

I preferred choosing my own subject. I remember we were told to write about an aeroplane ride. That stumped me, I had never seen aeroplanes and knew nothing about them. Though people may have been flying those first planes, it was not a subject discussed. In Shakespeare Cottage, we were forbidden to read the newspaper, it was not for children.

I remember writing about A Tree, and when I went back into the classroom to collect my book of poems on the way to the Dining Hall, the Headmaster and another teacher were discussing my composition. I knew it was good because I liked it myself. I had this strange feeling when I read my work back, where did all these thoughts come from?

Art or drawing I hated. Nobody actually taught us to draw, I had no idea how to get dimensions and when a clock was stood on the teacher's table and we were told to draw it, I gazed in disbelief, boredom and hate. I made the round circle, stuck on some numbers and a pair of hands.

I remember a humorous incident in drawing. We were told to draw a bull chasing a boy through a paddock. At the desk in front of me sat a boy called Tommy Rouse, Tommy could draw without any effort and there I sat with a blank piece of paper. Joey White who was sitting next to Tommy started to giggle. I tapped Tommy on the shoulder and looked at his drawing and wondered why I hadn't thought of that.

Tommy had drawn the bull's head coming on to the paper and drawn a fence across the other side of the paper with the boy's backside disappearing off the paper. Our teacher had no sense of humour, he came over, looked and screwed it up and told Tommy to draw it properly.

I think he hated it because Tommy was showing initiative and also because he would wonder if this child was being funny at his expense. I shall never know why I received good marks for drawing.

9. SEW AND SEW

I think we all hated sewing and also the Sewing Teacher. Firstly, we were never allowed to talk in class and whereas most teachers took no notice of the whispering that always went on, the Sewing Teacher would not even permit this. Sometimes she would soften and allow various students to read books such as The Wind in the Willows, Charles Dickens and books of poems. For me, reading made sewing more tolerable.

We actually did very little each week. By the time each girl showed the teacher her work, or asked for advice, or had to unpick the work, it was a relief when the session was over. It always took so long to first go to the cupboard and get our work out, 'No talking', and then to pack our work up and put it in the cupboard, 'No talking'.

I do remember winning just once. We always had to do work with white material and it was so easy to get grubby. I was making a handkerchief, with drawn thread work. That means drawing five or six strands out of the cloth on each side of the handkerchief and then painstakingly with very fine thread and extra fine sewing needle gathering up five of these threads as if making a little bundle and neatly fixing it to the hem.

After you did one side of the handkerchief, it was taken to the teacher to be passed. For weeks the teacher made me unpick that work until the cloth became limp like rag and grey in colour. I was exasperated, what could I do, to lose sewing was impossible, I couldn't take it home, someone would see me and report me.

A daring thought came to me, I could put it down the lavatory. We

36

had a pan system and the pan was taken out and emptied every day and a clean one put in its place. When the time came to pack away my sewing, I hid it on my person, went back to my seat and waited to be dismissed. I fled to the toilet and dropped it in with lots of newspaper on top. The deed was done and I never dared tell anyone. I scared myself sick wondering if I could ever be found out.

The next sewing day arrived and we carried out the normal routine. I said to the teacher: "I'm sorry, Teacher, I can't find my sewing." She replied: "Go back and look for it, it can't be lost." In the end she came to look, but was unable to find it. I spent the whole lesson looking and suffering verbally from her the whole time. I was bored, half wished I hadn't got rid of it, but in the end I received a crisp new piece of material to start all over again.

I got rapped over the knuckles with a ruler many times and was sent outside for whispering, to await punishment either by her or to be sent to the Headmaster's class. The Headmaster saw me standing there one time and took me back into the classroom. He asked the teacher what it was all about and she told him. He said that he thought it was quite natural for children to talk and suggested we be allowed to talk quietly while waiting for her attention. I think this is how we were allowed to read books.

Most of our teachers were kindly. I remember a teacher saying to one of the boys, while we were waiting for assembly: "Go tell Florrie Brown FB stands for flea bite." The boy did so and I looked up to see the teacher thoroughly enjoying his little joke, after all I was only a flea bite.

I also remember another teacher, Mr Scanlon, who had a shocking temper and pupils hated being in his class. He took the class next to us when I was in the Headmaster's class. One day there was a tremendous commotion, naturally we all stood up and saw Mr Scanlon with a large swishing cane chasing one of the boys round his classroom. Mr Scanlon was red in the face and the Headmaster went in and restored order. The boy was brought into our class where the Headmaster announced that this boy had just won the round with his teacher and his reward was twelve cuts. After that incident Mr Scanlon left.

Music like poetry filled a void. I loved the sound of singing and the use of words. I remember the tuning fork to give us middle C and then to run up or down the scale to find the note we needed. I also still remember singing the scales and the words we used for the different ones: 'Peek a boo I see you, Hiding behind the door'; 'Three tin soldiers in a row, Bugle calls and off they go'; 'Toss a white feather up into the air'.

The scales were always drawn on the blackboard and I loved hearing about B flat, G sharp, or drawing treble clef or bass clef, and placing the crotchets and quavers and demi semiquavers. They all made such beautiful sounds.

I remember a great disappointment with singing lessons or music lessons as they were called. We had a woman teacher and she commenced the lesson this day by saying whoever got the most marks in class she would teach them the piano. On the board were drawn all the music symbols and questions were asked. Up shot my arm, in fact mine was the only one that shot up consistently and mine was the only name written on the blackboard.

"Florrie Brown, you have won, I shall teach you the piano."

I never had one lesson, I waited daily for lessons to happen until I realised they never would. I wondered whether she was told by Authority that she could not pick out one child for special lessons or whether she just did not mean it. I shall never know for she never spoke to me about it.

10. CONCERT HIGHLIGHTS

Concerts were a highlight for me, these were apart from the ones performed outside Fairbridge. It was so easy for Authority to train us because it was part of our life. You turned up for practice at the required times and the Cottage Mother was responsible for your attendance. If you were being punished for anything, that had to wait until practice for sport or the concert had been completed.

To be selected to perform we would line up in a semicircle on our class stage and sing whatever we had been given. The teacher went from class to class and would walk down the rows placing his ear to our mouth, and then tap us on the shoulder.

Most of our concerts were religious Cantatas and nearly everything we did had a moral attached. I hated this moralising and in adult years when I taught Religious Instruction, I would never draw a moral from the story but leave it to speak for itself.

One of the Cantatas we performed was Soot and the Fairies, which extolled the virtues of soap and a pure clean mind. Captain Soot and his gang of dirty children sang a song that mirrored my way of thinking then and for many years to come.

Chorus:
Mumble mumble moan
Misery mercy me
All the time is wear and tear
Life is but a poor affair
Mumble mumble moan
Misery mercy me
Mercy mercy misery mercy me.

Verse:
It's early to bed and it's early to rise
and I hate to go early to bed Oh
I'd fly to the moon if I had a balloon
I'd stroll to the pole if I could Oh

There were other songs in the same miserable vein, such as
sulking was 'a little black dog on your back'. Another song I
remember singing that was full of morals was:

Come pretty children listen to a song
Song of a gay coquette
Someone had admired it,
Someone had inspired it
Calling it a pretty pet
But down in the valley
Hidden by the green
A dear little lily bloomed unseen
Now which of the two would you rather have been
The rose or the lily that bloomed unseen
We should answer why the lily
For roses must see the sun or fade
But lilies blossom in the shade.

As I was the principal singer, my Cottage Mother would use the
words in these songs against me, especially reminding me about
the lily that bloomed unseen and not to get 'too big for my boots'.
These concerts would be finally acted out on the Dining Hall stage
and our Cottage Mothers were able to observe us.

Even the natural exhilaration I should have received from this, for I
loved acting as well as singing and poetry, was kept shut down
tightly under a lid. Ability might be recognised as pride for the
school, individually it was never encouraged as a talent. But if you
were a failure, such as me with spelling, you were made to feel it.
When I was in the Headmaster's class, one of the boys was having

great difficulty learning. The Headmaster was discussing the words 'sane' and 'insane'. After explaining the meanings, he turned to this boy and asked him: "Are you sane or insane?" The boy thought for a while and, thinking he had the correct answer, replied: "Insane, Sir."

The whole class roared with laughter and they were allowed to go on while that poor kid stood there confused, unable to comprehend what had been to everyone else so funny. I thought it was cruel and always felt Mr Healey should not have allowed the class to enjoy another person's discomfiture.

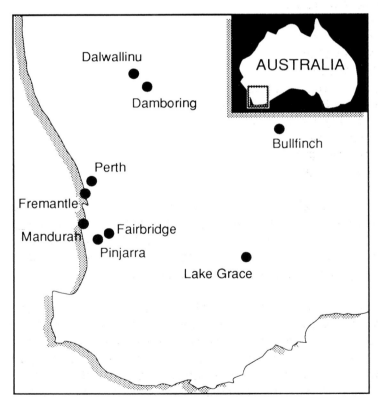

The area of Western Australia which Flo knew

Graphic by Alan Bott

I always looked forward to sports of all kinds and sports day. We didn't compete in class teams but factions or houses, Red, White, Blue and Gold. I was in Red as was Hilda Green, my closest rival, Ann Phillips whom I could never beat was in Gold. We competed as sub Juniors, Juniors and Seniors.

Luckily Ann was a year older so every other year I had a chance to win the medal that was presented at the close of school ceremony held in the Dining Hall. All your sporting wins/marks went to the house total though individual scores were kept to determine the champions.

Scores were three points for a win, two for a second and one for a third. In the girls' races it was Red first and second, either Hilda or me, and third to Blue and Jeannie Lucas. Every alternate year the pattern would be Gold first to Ann, with Red second and third, Hilda or me.

I practised every day at playtime for sports day. The events were racing fifty yards (46 metres), seventy five yards, hundred yards and two hundred and twenty yards. One year the girls also ran the four hundred and forty but too many ended up distressed and it was never run again.

I came first or second in that race and girls were collapsing everywhere, my legs were shaking like jelly from the exertion. I was sorry the race was stopped, maybe all we needed was practice for the distance.

I competed in every event, skipping race, three legged race with

42

Hilda, high jump, long jump, hop, step and jump, and potato race where potatoes were laid in a line away from you and you had to run to the furthest one, pick it up and run back to the start, and so on till they were all collected.

Our names would be called out and we would line up for the events. My second year as a sub Junior I was competing against Hilda, we were too young then to keep our individual scores but we were running neck and neck and sometimes even tied in a race.

It was a great competition and I was so excited thinking I had won the medal. Hilda on the other hand kept telling me she had won it but I would have none of that. Come the great night of the medal presentation and the sub Junior winner was Hilda, she'd beaten me by half a point. How I wished I could have gone back on the sports field and won another point.

My first race as a Junior was against Ann. Now Ann's legs were as long as mine were short and she covered that ground like greased lightning. I remember the nervous tension as I lined up to compete. I overheard some teachers betting on who they thought would win.

One said: "Well, I'm backing 'Titch' here." The other replied: "But look at Ann, such long legs, she'll never beat her." The first teacher said: "One day she will, I'm still backing 'Titch'."

I was getting more and more nervous and had to keep running to the lavatory while waiting for the race to start, it was a wonder I had any energy left. Finally the race, and after all the races that day, Ann won the Junior medal but it was only just. I was always spurred on against Ann and tried that much harder to beat her.

The following year it was Hilda and I with Jeannie. I managed to win every race, I jumped my own height in the high jump and I won the Junior medal. On the back of the thin silver medal is written, 'F.F.S Junior Athlete Florence Brown 1933'. A year later Ann won again and then left school, but I had also left school before sports day took place the year after that.

Although they let me compete (I was still at Fairbridge, doing my training), I had grown as plump as I was long and my body was too heavy to obey me. I had nightmares about this for years afterwards, trying to run in my dreams and my feet were stuck to the ground.

When we competed against children from other schools, some of the girls wore spiked running shoes but we still ran barefooted. I was taken away to an interschool sports competition and expected to perform well. I didn't have a chance, they were trained runners, wore the right shoes and knew the starting rules. I finished in the middle of the bunch.

I remember a conversation between the Sports Master and another male teacher who had accompanied us, the Sports Master said we were at a disadvantage and they would not take us again. The competition was a terrible strain and all for nothing.

We did not have a school uniform, we went to school in singlet, bloomers and a cotton dress, and in winter we also had a flannelette petticoat. We were dressed in the same awkward clothes for sports day.

We realised that with the high jump or long jump or anything to do with jumping, the boys would gather in a heap close to where we landed. I used to wonder about this until we learnt the awful truth, they could see what colour bloomers we were wearing and they would nudge one another as we cleared the hurdle and landed on the ground.

I suggested to the girls that on sports day we put on our bathers, like we did for paper chases, and throw our dress on top. I wore red woollen bathers, all our bathers were wool, and as I landed over the high jump bar I would say to the boys: "Red," and run off before they could reply, blushing as I did as I was being forward. It was a good solution and we were able to turn it against the boys rather than be embarrassed.

The boys at Fairbridge as far as I was concerned were like cheeky brothers, part of the set up. Sexual feelings never entered the brain or body. I was to pick out one of the boys as a favourite, a special friend, but this never advanced from holding hands on the way home from training in the evening and a desire to give a gift for Christmas or birthday.

I remember one incident where the girls got up to mischief behind the lavatories. Someone with a little more curiosity than me told us that boys were different from us and we decided to test this theory. One of the more daring among us managed to entice one of the very young boys, he was probably seven or eight, and there behind the lavatory his trousers were pulled down and there was his little penis for us all to see.

We had a good look and then pulling up his pants, he was warned about saying anything. We ran a real risk, it would have only required one girl to tell her Cottage Mother and we would all have been in serious trouble.

12. SEX AND THE STOREKEEPER

The corner store was visible as soon as you entered Fairbridge. There was a storekeeper, I don't know whether he owned or leased the shop or whether he was paid wages to run the store, but to me he was just another person in Authority.

I was never certain about how the school functioned. I was there to be looked after, to do as I was told, not to question any command, to avoid at all costs being reported for a misdemeanour, be trained to go out to work and finally marry and produce children.

I understand the Cottage Mothers were paid twenty five shillings per week and their keep but whether they were able to run up an account at the corner store, I am uncertain. When it was my duty to go to the store, my Cottage Mother would give me a list of groceries and sometimes I was given money to pay for some of the items.

I remember a funny obsession she had. When I had to buy kerosene from the store, the kerosene was pumped into a brown bottle and she insisted I took a roll of newspaper to wrap up the bottle just in case someone thought it was a bottle of beer. For years later this obsession fixed itself in my mind and I could never buy anything for myself in a brown bottle that resembled a bottle of beer.

The Storekeeper was kind, in fact very warm and friendly and we often received a lollipop for doing the messages. Unfortunately, his love for girls was expressed in sexual play. I was very lucky for he never asked me (or if he did I had not accepted) to go behind the counter to him, though I remember him holding a girl in front of him and rubbing his hands over the front of her clothes while still speaking to me. I interpreted this as being kind and loving. Eventually a girl must have told her Cottage Mother and the Storekeeper was discharged, it caused quite a hush through the whole place.

The sadness was that he had a beautiful voice and used to sing solos regularly in church. I enjoyed hearing him and especially because his choruses seemed to be based on being 'rescued from the mire' by a loving Jesus. I was waiting to be rescued by the same loving Jesus, and I can imagine now what that Storekeeper's plea was all about.

Shakespeare Cottage, showing the balcony from which the girls climbed down by rope for fire drill

13. CLASSROOM CLEANER

I was given the task of cleaning the classroom when I was in the Headmaster's class. You did the job for a month at a time and were paid 3d a month.

It consisted of sweeping the floor, dusting the desks and seeing the blackboards were wiped clean and fresh chalk was put out. I never minded cleaning the blackboards though I had to stand on a chair to reach the top. Naturally it was an after school task but we would not have been permitted to be home late.

There were two prerequisites for this task; firstly, we had to be trusted, perhaps it was thought we might steal something like chalk or a pencil or look at school papers. Secondly, at the end of the month we had to go to the Headmaster and ask for our pay of 3d and this was beyond me.

The first time I cleaned the classroom I was excited about earning the 3d, and remember waiting and waiting for Mr Healey to pay me. Then one day he said: "Florrie, did I pay you for the cleaning?"

"No, Sir," I said.

"Why didn't you come and ask me for your money?" he asked. I couldn't answer him, I had just assumed I would be paid and never imagined I would have to ask for it, somehow I couldn't see myself going to him and saying: "Please, Sir, may I have my 3d for cleaning the classroom."

I never could ask for that money. It felt like Oliver Twist asking for more. There was something bigger than I inside me that said you

48

shouldn't have to ask for something that is yours. It should be given to you. Usually after making me wait for some time I was paid, it was the one thing that spoilt for me cleaning of the classroom.

Another of my tasks in the Headmaster's class was stocktaking. Again you had to be trusted, this was the criterion behind everything and because of this you never worked quietly. I learnt to bump boxes of chalk as I was counting or hit writing pads as if I was removing dust, I managed to drop a pencil or two, anything to make a noise so Authority didn't say: "It's quiet in there, what's going on?"

I liked stocktaking as I was required to think and liked organising, anything that let me plan for myself and allowed a few moments for self development. I must have been good at this task for it to rate a mention in my school reports. I remember I was called on to stocktake each time it was required. Mr Healey would also pick me to run his messages, a blessed relief from class.

Looking back I feel the Headmaster was trying to get me to develop my natural self, what he didn't understand was that I didn't really know who I was, and how much and how far I could go without bringing the wrath of someone in charge or even the verbal bullying of the other children.

I don't know if they ever realised we had to fit into a system, or maybe they did and were trying to help us break away, at least in our mind. Because the school was State run it had more freedom than our home life, provided no one carried tales home from school.

The Headmaster, Mr Healey, is the one teacher I remember for quite a few reasons. I was now a teenager and my thoughts and behaviour were changing. My body was developing, I had begun to menstruate at the age of eleven. My whole personality was changing, though I could never express my thoughts in any type of discussion, they were all there bottled up inside my brain.

Mr Healey had been a soldier in the 1914-18 war and had suffered a war wound. A bullet had gone through both legs just up from the ankle. He was often in great pain and then was very short tempered in class and would often sit in a desk near the back with his feet stretched out in the aisle to conduct the lesson, usually different students going to the platform and giving impromptu talks.

Sometimes the student he called out was sitting behind him and this student in his hurry to obey rushed past too quickly and accidentally bumped Mr Healey's legs. He would call out in pain and his agony was distressing to watch. The person responsible would feel terrible and it would be quite a few moments before Mr Healey would be able to carry on. Many a lesson he gave ended up being about his life at war.

Another picture I have of that classroom was of a boy who used to have epileptic fits and somehow they seemed to coincide whenever Mr Healey took himself to the back of the classroom. Suddenly the commotion started, Ted would be in the aisle writhing around on the floor. Mr Healey would call out to one of the boys, who would get a teaspoon to put into Ted's mouth so he didn't swallow his tongue and watch him to see he didn't hit his head on the iron legs of the desk. When the fit had passed he would assist Ted to recover.

It was such a usual occurrence that after the first shock of the attack Mr Healey would carry on with the lesson, knowing Ted was being watched.

When I was almost seventeen, I was to meet Ted in Perth (where I was working) while he was waiting to catch a train to a job in the country. We went to the pictures but when his train time arrived the show wasn't over so I let him go alone. During the show, Ted gave me an expensive gift of a watch, written on the back was: 'To Florrie from Ted'. The watch is still in my family. How selfish and callous is youth.

I remember Mr Healey as stern but basically fair. He had a wife but no children and he and his wife tried to help one of our girls, Doris, who was a clever student to further her education.[5]

She and I were both hoping we might go on to further education.[6] It was an almost impossible task. My Cottage Mother, Miss Kittell, wanted me to, I wanted to be a Kindergarten teacher, I really loved teaching children. But when I met Mr Healey with my Cottage Mother he said I did not have the intelligence of the average Australian.

Those words sank so deeply into my being that I was to be well into my fifties before I began to challenge the untruth and the handicap those words laid on me. I was offered no extra tuition, no alternative education, was I truly brought down a peg or two, I was so very embarrassed by that statement.

---

[5] Tempe Woods wrote that 'every child who has entered some field of interest to himself has been struggled for by some adult member of staff'.
[6] She wrote to Flo in 1997, saying that she won a scholarship to Bunbury High School but was not allowed to take it up, being told that the farm school 'couldn't benefit one child over the other'. Another Old Fairbridgian wrote, also in 1997, that he attended Bunbury High from 1928-32.

After school chores commenced immediately on arriving in the cottage. These consisted of many activities, some tailored to the age of the child. I would run inside and in winter time hang my coat on the hook in the laundry, throw on a pinafore over my clothes and get started.

We had a garden competition every year and this meant constant weeding. There were no lawns between our garden beds, it was all neatly raked gravel and not one weed was permitted to pop its head up through that gravel.

To make this job tolerable, I would kneel on a hessian wheat bag (the gravel still hurt though) and then, stretching my arms as far as I could, I would draw my first square into four squares and place one large stone in the corner of each square. This stone became the teacher in the class and I would play schools as I weeded.

This way the chore would get done, the time would pass and my weeding would be inspected and passed. My only real suffering was my sore knees as I slid them across the ground. This job was done completely on my own so that I could not waste any time talking.

A shared job was going to the dairy paddocks to collect manure for the garden. I remember one frightening incident with Jeannie Lucas. We fetched the wheelbarrow and spade and together set off. We pushed the barrow along the top road and into the bush that skirted the side fence, looking anxiously for the bull that we knew lived in the paddocks. We usually made sure we were not wearing red for we truly believed the story of the bull chasing you if you wore that colour. This particular day I was wearing red and we worked ourselves up into a frightened state and as we reached the gate to go through with our barrow, a thunderous sound rang out.

We stood still literally stuck to the ground and clung to each other. Coming before us at great speed were two large draught horses pulling a dray mounted on large rubber wheels, bolting from whatever had frightened them. Our wheelbarrow was still at the iron gate and as the horses hit the gate the dray became tangled up in the wire fence and our barrow was pushed away.

Suddenly a large man appeared and belted into the horses in an uncontrolled rage, the horses rearing up in fear. Jeannie and I were still standing and watching. The horses became subdued and the man set about extricating them from the dray. He saw us and angrily pushed the wheelbarrow towards us.

We were unable to get through the gate and turned slowly home with not one dollop of manure collected. Perhaps I should not have worn red. We reported the incident to our Cottage Mother. Later we learnt that this man was discharged because of his temper and cruelty to horses. We did collect manure again but were always fearful of seeing the bolting horses.

Another job was chopping wood and I learnt to split wood very well. I don't remember any of us ever injuring ourselves with the axe but you were walloped by pieces of wood flying in the air if you became a little careless. The wood locker was set in the kitchen, two doors opening outside for filling and doors opening inside for removing. The job was finished when the locker was full.

We also had to light the copper fire for the bathwater and there were some do's and don'ts about this job which sometimes I deliberately forgot. The blackboy when it is old makes wonderful kindling. The danger was its habit of getting very sticky when burning up and of spitting out of the fire for quite a few inches.

One of our rules when lighting the fire was not to sit in front of it. Of course I did on most occasions, provided I knew my Cottage Mother was not likely to walk through the laundry. Paper, a few twigs, a good sprinkling of blackboy pieces and then the match, it was good to feel the warm glow on a cold day.

Sometimes it required a good blowing to get going and then forgetting completely except the contentment of watching the fire take hold, I would sit cross legged feeding the gentle flame. Suddenly bang, crackle and out would fly a piece of flaming blackboy and if I wasn't quick enough it would land on my leg.

One day a piece stuck on my shinbone, but fortunately it was only a small piece because even that burnt and stung. I pulled it off and wiped my leg clean and had to put up with the agony till the sting went.

There was no use running to my Cottage Mother as I wasn't supposed to be sitting in front of the fire. I still had to feed the growing flame although the heat stung my leg. Once the fire was strong enough to take thicker chunks of wood and the water was on its way to getting hot, my job was to regularly check and keep the fire going.

The copper was in the corner of the laundry against the bathroom wall. When I first arrived at the cottage I would have to dip a kerosene bucket into the copper of boiling water and carry it into the bathroom and tip it into the bath, carrying enough bucket loads till the bath was ready.

It was very awkward and very dangerous, but it was not until my Cottage Mother observed me carrying out this task that the danger of scalding was considered. Miss Kittell reported her concern to the Chairman of the Fairbridge Perth Society, Mr Joyner. He came to our cottage to assess the problem himself and agreed it was unsafe. The solution was to cut a hole in the laundry wall right beside the copper and a tin chute was fitted snugly into the opening and came out over the bath. From then I only had to use a large dipper to pour the boiling water into the chute.

Our bath and laundry troughs were made of rough stone, there was no smooth finish even in the bath. You can imagine how our bottoms felt and even though we would try to sit on our flannels it was still painful. The day Mr Joyner inspected the cottage he asked Miss Kittell about the rough bath and how she found it.

It must have been terrible for her as she was in her sixties and would also have had difficulty getting in and out of the deep trough. She must have told him and we were given a new enamel bath. While the children would not have been considered, at least our Cottage Mother was.

The old bath was taken outside into the garden. Mr Joyner was very excited at the joy the new bath had created and suggested we turn the old bath into a goldfish pond. He told us how to feed goldfish and that they become quite tame. We had to cover the top of the bath with fine wire netting because the kookaburras decided they also liked goldfish.

One of my jobs for a while was to feed the goldfish each evening, dampening what looked like a mixture of rolled oats into a small ball and dropping these into the bath pond.

With the stone bath, cleaning consisted of scrubbing hard with a very rough brush, damaging your skin in the process. The enamel bath was a much harder task, as it had to look each day as if seventeen children and a Cottage Mother had not been through it.

The evening meal, tea, was eaten in the cottages, unlike breakfast and dinner. Preparation involved two of us, the kitchen table had to be set, the stove lighted and the meal cooked.

Sometimes we had sausages and the delight of those sausages still remains with me. We would roll them in flour and having already placed a baking dish with some dripping in the oven, we would wait for it to melt the hot oil and then placing the sausages in the dish, two per person, we would return the dish to the oven and lovingly turn them at intervals until they were really crisp.

I can't remember having anything else with them but bread and dripping, milk to drink and finishing off with bread and jam.

For the Cottage Mother, her tea was put on a tray, whatever she ordered and her teapot, warmed before adding boiling water to the tea leaves and drawn for five minutes, and served with her special china cup on her special linen tray cloth. All this was done exactly as she had shown us.

Some nights we had fried bread, lovely thick hunks of bread dipped into a plate of milk before being placed in heated fat, spitting and protesting till crisp and brown on both sides. The bread was then put in the oven to keep warm until enough was done, many pieces were cooked at once using the large baking dish for frying.

Puff daloons were another dish we cooked in boiling fat. They were a dough of self raising flour shaped into round balls and dropped into the fat, we watched them quickly form into large puffs which were then rolled in sugar and eaten. Quite often tea was bread and milk followed by bread and jam or dripping. Sometimes we had whipped cream, oh delicious joy piled on bread and jam. A variation was bread and jam with a little milk on top of the jam.

Jam was bought in long thin 28 lb (13 kg) tins, I think we received monthly orders of food for our evening meals. The deliveries occurred while we were at school. The tin would be opened with the usual tin opener and oh those rough edges, the tin stood in a tray of water to protect the jam from the ants.

If you were on duty and had to open the tin and forgot to stand the tin in water or forgot to check the water hadn't dried up, in no time the tin would be full of ants. The ants were impossible to remove but every bit of jam had to be eaten before we received a new tin. I used to try to take out as many ants as I could but it was an impossible task and the jam never lost the flavour of ants.

Dripping was a tasty spread if it was full of the flavour of baked sausages and the brown jelly had formed at the bottom of the dripping. The smell of new dripping being melted down or being used for the first time, however, turned my stomach. Even though all this hot fat was used for cooking, I don't recall anyone being burnt.

Washing up is hard to recall, even though seventeen girls were fed every night there was only one enamel plate and cup per person, a knife and teaspoon. We didn't have tablecloths, the table was kept scrubbed white with Bon Ami or bath brick. Bon Ami was white and shaped like a square brick, bath brick was greyish sand in colour. There was no running hot water, the hot water was boiled on the stove in large iron kettles or carried to the sink from the boiler (preserving pan).

Sewing for the Royal Perth Show, writing letters to England, patching clothes and running errands for the Cottage Mother were all after school chores. These tasks took us up to tea and after tea it was bathtime. If we had any time over, that was our own free time. It might be spent in the sitting room where Miss Kittell would be sitting in her chair and the youngest children would sit on the floor around her talking.

As I got older I would sit cross legged on the lockers and read. Sometimes the older girls would put on an impromptu concert for Miss Kittell for a reward, she often had lollies (hard sweets that took lovely ages to suck) hidden behind the curtain in her bedroom and we would receive one each.

The younger girls would be in bed by 7 pm and we would kneel down beside our beds and say our prayers:

Now I lay me down to sleep
I pray the Lord my soul to keep
If I should die before I wake
I pray the Lord my soul to take.

This prayer was rattled off with no meaning, I certainly never expected to die before I waked. We then quickly said the Lord's Prayer and jumped into bed and snuggled down. While nobody supervised prayers, no one thought of missing them however cold it was. Once in bed, in fact once in the dormitory, there was no talking on fear of the cane. At 8 pm the bugle sounded again.

Day is done, gone the sun
From the sea, from the hills, from the sky
All is well, sweetly rest
God is nigh.

16. ENTERTAINING MISS KITTELL

Plaistowes, the chocolate people, and though I didn't know it then I was to work for them for two years, gave our Cottage Mother a very large tin of toffee de luxe to share among us all.

The only way we could score a toffee was to put on a concert for the night. I liked to try my hand at anything but Ann, who was tall and willowy against me who was short and plumpish, was very good at dancing. She made up her own dances as she went along, I can still see her arms waving high above her head and her legs quietly stepping and flinging high in the air.

She asked me to dance with her and I tried to copy her steps, the rest of the girls would be humming and clapping their hands to whatever music Ann wanted. I loved it and when we finished, Miss Kittell would say to Ann how graceful she was and turning to me would say: "Poor Florrie, like a bag of potatoes, will never make a dancer."

I would recite or sing or we would all sing to 'Miss' but to me the highlight was Ann's dancing and me being asked to dance with her. As a wee tot in Barnardo's, I had been in the Baby Drillers and had gone to the Albert Hall with a number of other girls to dance and sing and I tried to show the other girls in my cottage these dances. Some of us would dance to these tunes:

Hurrah Hurrah what merry little maids we are
We dance and sing as happy as can be
One and a two and a three and a four and a five six seven eight
(repeated once as we skipped first one way and then danced in a circle).

Then, a separate song, we pretended we were dancing with boys:

Will you please be my partner and dance in a ring
With our hands joined together, we will merrily sing
First we'll step forward and then we'll step back
and dance in a ring, we'll go clippetty clap.

Then the boys leave their partners and come back again
Then the girls follow after and just do the same
Then my dear partner I'll wish you good day
Then my dear partner may dance as you may.

I could only have been about six when I performed at the Albert Hall yet I've never forgotten the dance or the words or the music. Being so small, I was always able to get the younger girls to dance with me. Music of all sorts I loved and dancing is the body's way of expressing music. A few of the other girls would do their bit entertaining but mostly in community singing.

Bedtime arrived and we waited expectantly to be rewarded. Miss Kittell would let the first of us say goodnight and I would think, oh no reward tonight, when she would say: "I nearly forgot, wait there a moment."

I knew what was happening, just as we all did, that large tin of toffee de luxe was coming out and we all rapturously were given one. That toffee took such a gorgeous long time to chew in the mouth as it stuck sweetly all over your teeth, on the roof of your mouth and your tongue pushed and shoved it till not a skerrick was left, only the juicy saliva.

Those toffee de luxe sat for a long time in the tin behind the curtain in Miss Kittell's room. For one of the girls in particular, she must have had a sweet tooth, the agony of waiting for one toffee to be doled out was too much and she decided she would steal a handful of them. We all knew because she told one of the other girls, who then had to tell other girls and like wildfire it spread through the cottage. I was really scared for stealing was not worth getting caught out.

Now to protect herself, she started giving out these toffees and once you had eaten one your crime was equal to that of the girl who stole. Finally, she came to me. "Topsy," she said, "have a toffee." My whole being asked for that toffee but I refused and she called me some nasty names.

For a while the crime went unnoticed and so she stole some more. She must have known that Miss Kittell would notice and of course finally it was discovered. It took a while before she admitted to stealing the toffees and naturally all the other girls that shared in the delights were also thrashed. I was relieved, as my fear of thrashing was stronger than my deep want of toffee.

As a consequence, most of us suffered because there were now fewer toffees to hand out.

I was called 'Topsy' by a lot of my school mates because I had played the part of Topsy in Uncle Tom's Cabin. It was one play we did that I shall never forget for apart from my skin being made black, I think it was from burnt cork, and other parts of the body like legs and arms were covered in black stockings, I remember the parts that I truly meant as I said them:

I nedder had a mother,
I nedder had a father,
I was just born.

In the production, a necklace that Topsy was accused of stealing I had to shove up my sleeve. Topsy of course had not stolen it. I forget whether it was planted on her or it catches in her clothing. I remember as I played the part feeling the fear of Topsy and expecting any moment to be her and be punished for her crime.

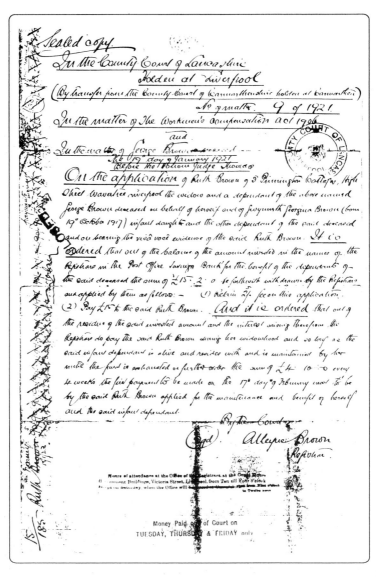

Sealed copy

In the County Court of Lancashire
Holden at Liverpool
(By transfer from the County Court of Carmarthenshire holden at Carmarthen)
No. of matter 9 of 1921

In the matter of The Workmen's Compensation Act 1906
and
In the matter of George Brown deceased.

The 19th day of January 1921
Before the Robins Judge Thomas

On the application of Ruth Brown of 8 Pimington Cottages, High Street Wavertree Liverpool the widow and a dependant of the above named George Brown deceased on behalf of herself and of Gwyneth Georgina Brown (born 19th October 1917) infant daughter and the other dependant of the said deceased and on hearing the viva voce evidence of the said Ruth Brown. It is ordered that out of the balance of the amount invested in the names of the Registrars in the Post Office Savings Bank for the benefit of the dependants of the said deceased the sum of £15. 2. 0 be forthwith withdrawn by the Registrars and applied by them as follows: — (1) Retain 2/- fee on this application. (2) Pay £15 to the said Ruth Brown. And it is ordered that out of the residue of the said invested amount and the interest arising therefrom the Registrars do pay the said Ruth Brown during her widowhood and so long as the said infant dependant is alive and resides with and is maintained by her until the fund is exhausted or further order the sum of £4 10 0 every 4 weeks the first payment to be made on the 17th day of February next to be by the said Ruth Brown applied for the maintenance and benefit of herself and the said infant dependant.

By the Court
(Sgd). Alleyne Brown
Registrar

Hours of attendance at the Office of the Registrars at the Court House Government Buildings, Victoria Street, Liverpool, from Ten till Four o'clock except on Saturday when the Office will be open from Nine o'clock to Twelve noon

Money Paid out of Court on
TUESDAY, THURSDAY & FRIDAY only

*Flo's mother's compensation order, transferred
to Liverpool from Carmarthen*

I would often cry for her as I did also for the character in the book A Basket of Flowers. This was a story about a young girl, working as a domestic in a wealthy home, being accused of stealing a brooch and being put in prison. I can still vividly see the picture of the wan face peering out through the bars.

A jackdaw had taken it and when its nest fell out of the tree the brooch was found. Then all was forgiven but nobody was able to make up for the agony of disgrace and injustice. I wasn't the only girl who read that book with tears streaming down her face.

During my time at Fairbridge I was called many things including 'stuck up' when I tried to get away on my own and think for myself. It was asked: "Who do you think you are?" When I tried to understand myself, I was told that I was swollen headed.

If perhaps some visitor had praised my recitation and later I had neglected my household chores (neglect meaning it didn't pass inspection and could mean one smear on a cleaned window), I was cast as a 'show off' because of my ability to act and sing and would be taunted with it if other girls or my Cottage Mother wanted to hurt me. Due to my ability to make a full Court curtsy and to recite whenever Royalty or important visitors came to Fairbridge, I would be brought before them to perform.

It was the same poem every time, though I learnt others, I was never allowed to change and it started: 'Great wide and beautiful wonderful world, With the wonderful waters around you curled'.

I learnt very early that I never said no to any request or I would be punished. I could not act shy even if I was nervous or not feeling well. But another seed was sown in my mind, that you must never say: "No" when asked to do anything you were capable of doing. This used to exasperate me as an adult, when pianists would put on a great performance about not being able to play and then after much protest they finally did.

17. DANCING, PT AND PICTURE SHOWS

Every hour of our day and evening was filled with activity. My life was a timetable, all this routine being to keep the devil away.

Dancing lessons involved boys' and girls' cottages to ensure everybody had a partner. The Sports Master was in charge and there was a pianist and often the Head Matron, a nasty natured person, was there overseeing our behaviour.

Always in the back of their minds was the thought that a boy and girl would couple up and disappear and get up to that wicked mischief they worried about. But nobody became pregnant, the whole of Fairbridge would have been told by the Principal had this happened.

I remember him telling us during his lectures before breakfast that girls who 'got into trouble', ie pregnant outside of marriage, in the outside world was one in ten but the Fairbridge average was much lower and that he was pleased with us. It is a wonder with the sudden freedom and with a false feeling of being loved, and in some cases extreme ignorance, that we didn't 'get into trouble'.[7]

Our dancing lessons had rules too, no dancing twice with the same boy and if by any chance you tried to break this rule, hoping you hadn't been noticed, the boy was sent to sit out the rest of the lesson behind the piano. The boy was the one punished because we girls were taught that we never said: "No" to the boy who asked

---

[7] Geoffrey Thomas reported that sex education was 'dealt with, if at all, in a very haphazard way'. He thought that it was very important given the mixed community and often earlier maturity brought by the climate. "It would stop a lot of unpleasantness on the Farm and might well prevent some tragedies among the Old Fairbridgians, especially the O.F. girls."

64

to partner us. Each dance was announced by the Sports Master, the Gay Gordons, barn dance, waltz etc.

He had a cow bell which he would ring and the boys would get up, they were made to sit at the other end of the hall, and collect a partner who sat with equal trepidation – we were all nervous – wondering who was going to ask her.

Once on the floor, our instructor would ring the cow bell if the dance wasn't being done correctly. You could all hear him sing out: "Tommy, stop pumping the handle," as some of the boys thought it great fun and absolutely correct to pump the arm holding the girl's hand up and down like a lever. If the boy didn't stop, behind the piano he went and the lass had to sit out for want of a partner.

That cow bell seemed to be ringing all the time: "Johnnie, you've danced twice with the same girl, behind the piano with you," or "Maryanne, what's wrong with you, can't you dance tonight? Come and sit down with me."

I loved dancing, in particular the grace of the circular waltz and the vitality of the gavotte. I remember once the Colonel walked in while we were doing the waltz and came straight over to me and, asking my partner, swept me up in his one arm and waltzed with me the whole way round, returning me to my partner. That was a real thrill, high, high up in the air I was, twirling around with great gusto, so small and light, I would have been no weight to him.

When dance time was over, we girls were dismissed first and told what streets we were to walk along, the boys were dismissed about five minutes later and they were told to walk along a different street. It didn't matter which way we walked, there was always a junction where the streets met and we would wait there till the boys caught up. Then shyly if I had a special boy, I would hold hands until nearly home and then laughing goodnight would run to my cottage.

I also enjoyed physical training. This was conducted by cottages, not mixed, and took the form of activities such as the English song (it was called that because we learnt it in England):

Sheep sheep come home (sung by the wolf)
We are afraid (we would reply)
What of (the wolf)
The wolf etc
The wolf has gone to Devonshire
and won't be back etc
So sheep sheep come home. . . .

At this moment, everybody jumped off the forms on which we were standing and flew to the other end of the hall, dodging and swirling to avoid being caught by the wolf. If you were caught you joined the mob.

Other activities included exercises such as knee bends, touching toes, marching, running on the spot, skipping. We used dumb bells and did some vaulting. The boys naturally would have harder tasks physically, much of our activity was running or chasing or dodging. By the end of physical training I was always happily weary.

I think we had picture shows once a month, again held in the Dining Hall and also looked forward to. They were silent black and white pictures of Rin Tin Tin, of cowboys doing wonderful things, plenty of shooting, all sub titled, and we kids would hiss and boo (later sound movies came in).

We never had a show where the film didn't break down so the fun was in the noise we made waiting for it to start again, such as singing. Our noise often became too much for the adults running the show and we were made to stop. The breaks would occur more than once and we sometimes had to wait for another evening to see the rest of the film.

18. WEEKENDS

Weekends started the same as any other day except that after breakfast all the big chores had to be done. Every bit of the cottage was polished from top to bottom, the walls, the floors and the furniture.

We made the polish for the walls and furniture using beeswax, turpentine and methylated spirits. The beeswax was melted down and turpentine and methylated spirits whipped through till it resembled whipped cream. The cream really did its job, except any crack if the cream got well and truly in would leave a long white mark and it took something like a toothbrush to get it all out.

Not one bit of cream was allowed to show or it meant doing it all over again.

The floors were done with kerosene and sump oil, a visitor once remarked that it would go up with a bang if a fire started. You had the mixture in a cut down kerosene tin and, on your hands and knees with a cloth, spread it all over the floor, then the whole lot was polished the same way, two girls to a floor.

We learnt a way of polishing but watch out if you were caught. One girl would sit on the polishing cloth for the final polish and the other girl, using the cloth like a cart, would pull her hard across the floor. Of course taking it in turns it was quite fun and did the job better than patch by patch on hands and knees.

When you were finished you got to the doorway and, lying flat, you looked across the surface of the floor because if you left one smear behind it was back to do the whole job.

One job I had was to clean the copper, with a mixture of kerosene and bath brick made into a paste. This was smeared all over the copper rubbing very hard and then came the job of polishing it off. How that copper gleamed, it shone. But if even a speck, enough to cover a small button, was missed, it had to be cleaned again.

In the kitchen not a grease stain was to be seen, the stove was thoroughly polished with black lead until the steel bits glowed bright. The bath had a thorough clean and shone without a mark. The table top in the sitting room was as shiny clear as a mirror, the back steps were scrubbed, the lavatory was scrubbed with phenyl, the windows were cleaned, even the dormitory windows.

We learnt to clean these high windows by sitting on the sill and pulling the window down to secure our bodies. I quite enjoyed this task but it gives me the shivers to think of it now. The stairs and banisters were well polished, especially the rail, for sliding down the banisters (while nobody was watching) was a grand pastime. All our work was inspected by Miss Kittell.

Following the clean up, we had to take medicine, this was a weekly ritual whether required or not. It could have been castor oil (before this was banned except on the Doctor's or Sister's authority), Epsom salts, senna tea, liquorice powder, all these were hard to swallow, especially the castor oil.

If you were unlucky enough to vomit back your first dose, another was served. Then we lined up for sulphur and treacle, cod liver oil and malt. I can still feel that mess stuck in my mouth, I tried hard to down it with one large swallow and it took all my willpower to control my stomach's desire to expel it. This ritual was always conducted on the back door steps, perhaps just in case someone did vomit.

After medicine, our hair was checked for lice. Lice were considered a sign of filth and low breeding and though everything was scrubbed from top to bottom, including ourselves, we as orphans were considered to be carriers. Head inspection involved use of a toothcomb, a small flat almost square comb with teeth either side, and a saucer of kerosene. The comb was dipped and then slowly, with regular dipping, combed through the scalp. In the wrong hands this was a painful experience.

If by chance lice were found, and they were sometimes on those recently arrived by ship from England, the hair was completely shaved off. It was a horrible disgrace. It never happened to me at Fairbridge but at Barnardo's in England your hair was shaved off automatically on arrival.

Saturday was also the day of the fire drill, climbing over the balcony and holding on to a sailor's knotted rope, going down knot by knot, heart thumping, the knots spaced just far enough apart to allow us to do this. At first, it was frightfully scary but I grew to love it, I really thrived on it. It took only a few minutes to complete my turn but seventeen girls had to go through the whole procedure. The Sports Master was there watching with the Cottage Mother.

The rope exercise was performed only by the girls as the boys' cottages were bungalows. Sometimes it took all the skill of the Sports Master and the encouragement of the rest of us to get a few girls to step over the balcony, they were petrified. I don't recall the fire drill being put to use.

It was forbidden to climb down the rope except on fire drill. Even if Authority never saw you, there was always some girl to report on you or to hold it over your head like a blackmail threat, to be used when needed. This especially applied if they wanted you to take the blame for something they had done like stealing and they themselves didn't want to get punished.

Saturday afternoons consisted of organised sports. My main sport was hockey, I also played tennis and swam. We practised after school throughout the swimming months, basketball and Captain Ball (another ball game) were also played.

I was a good enough hockey player for my Sports Mistress Miss Phillips to tell me that if I was able to get a job in Perth, she would get me into the State team. This was another promise I looked forward eagerly to materialising but it never did, although I did get work in Perth. I usually played left wing because of my ability to run.

We took trips away to play teams outside of Fairbridge and these teams played return visits. We were a top team and won most of our games. During one trip to a place called Yarloop, I remember two incidents.

Yarloop and Fairbridge were tied on the score match draw (tied on the competition table) and Yarloop didn't want to be beaten by us. We travelled in a bus, the Fairbridge driver Frank Parry in charge and Miss Phillips sitting up in front with him. We were approaching Yarloop and had to cross a river by a bridge when Frank braked suddenly. Across the bridge in the path of the tyres were broken bottles.

The whole team piled out of the bus and, barefooted as usual, removed the glass. We arrived at Yarloop late, but not too late to forfeit the game, which had to be the reason behind the broken glass. The hockey field was on the side of a river built on natural rock and, to add to the danger, the pitch had a decided slope.

There was no time for anything but to start the game. Yarloop were hoping we would refuse to play. Miss Phillips gathered us together. "Play your best but I don't want any broken legs or arms, the pitch is dangerous, treat it as such," and then to me: "Don't try to run fast, you'll only slip and fall."

In one way I suppose it was lucky we weren't wearing shoes as it helped us not to slip but the rock surface was very hard. We drew the match and probably would have won on a better pitch. (We beat Yarloop on the return match played on our grass field at Fairbridge.) The match over, there was nothing friendly about this gathering, we piled back on the bus to return home.

A lot of the animosity shown by Yarloop was because we came from an institution and were also British. I was to encounter this attitude as I grew up and mixed with the outside world.

The return trip was as eventful as the rest of the day. Frank had to nurse the bus along to keep it going and he was cursing it all the time. As he grew more frustrated, we would sing.

In the midst of the gaiety I noticed a fire start inside the engine and sang out to Frank, who called: "Jump all of you." The bus cabin was formed by slats and I had already started to climb down to the road on the wrong side of the bus, into the path of oncoming traffic. Most girls got off the right side but all I could think of was the fire.

Frank was very brave as he lifted the bonnet and switched off the petrol line. I believe his reward was to be asked why he didn't let it burn so insurance could be claimed and a new bus purchased. We stayed beside the bus with Miss Phillips while Frank set off to inform Fairbridge. Another bus was sent to pick us up and we arrived back very tired and hungry but with an exciting tale to tell.

Another hockey match away from home we played at a place called Manjinup (lots of places ended in 'up' and we were told that this was an Aboriginal word for water). I was to play centre forward. We had only just started the game, bullying off and playing to get possession of the ball, when my opposing position gave my fourth finger an almighty whack against the hockey stick.

I was in great pain for she had split open my finger right beside the nail. Miss Phillips came over to look. "Sorry Florrie, you'll have to sit it out, if it gets better I'll send you back on." My finger should have been held together with plaster, instead I was given a piece of cloth to hold against it and it seemed forever before it stopped bleeding.

Miss Phillips thought it was a deliberate act to take me out of the game. I sat it out in great misery, the pain was bad enough, missing the game was worse, we lost that day. I still carry the scar and my fingernail never really grows but splits off at that spot.

We had a special uniform for sport when we travelled away from Fairbridge and when visiting teams came to play us. It was big and cumbersome and inhibited play but I always felt proud wearing it. The Fairbridge colours were brown and gold, brown for the earth and gold for the wheat.

The uniform consisted of a brown tunic top reaching to our knees and split on either side to our thighs. The splits were bound with gold ribbon and the pants were brown full sized bloomers with gold ribbon sewn up each side seam. The bloomers were particularly full on me and made me feel anchored to the ground, it was certainly not the best uniform for sport. The girls used to giggle and the boys used to snigger at us.

I started playing competition hockey at nine or ten years of age but later on our Doctor, who resided in Pinjarra, forbade any child under eleven to play hockey at all. He decided it wasn't good for us.

72

20. SWIMMING AMID LEECHES

The boys played soccer and I enjoyed watching them, bouncing the ball off their heads.

I was mediocre at tennis. I would have liked to be a good player but I could concentrate on one sport only and I couldn't find a racquet comfortable enough to hold in a firm grip. I was always trying different racquets, but I could never control the ball. When I made contact it would fly swiftly across the net but mostly out of court. My size was also a handicap.

Swimming was held by a few cottages at a time. The Sports Master supervised lessons which were held in the river. We were never allowed to walk into the water but had to jump off the bank. This wasn't easy for me because I had received a real scare shortly after arriving at Fairbridge.

It was the first lesson of the season. A log had fallen across the river where we were to swim and it had made a fairly deep hole, well, deep for someone like me who was only 3ft 5ins (1 m) tall. I was not able to swim but the Sports Master showed where to jump in, saying he would not let me drown.

I jumped and came up gasping for air, the Sports Master was there to hold me and start me dog paddling. After a few more jumps, I was allowed to play in the shallow water. One day I was jumping closer to the log and, when we non swimmers jumped, it was one at a time so the Sports Master could watch us. I jumped and was about to come up when someone deliberately landed on me, probably as a joke without realising the danger. The Sports Master saw it in time and rescued me but it was a fright I never forgot.

The river contained leeches, the long slimy black creatures would fasten on to me and it was difficult to pull them off. I had to grab a little river soil in my fingers to hold on to the leech to tug it off. They always left a trail of blood as they came away.

We were never permitted to swim on our own because the river used to flood and all sorts of logs would be washed downstream. Until the river was inspected it was out of bounds and I never heard of any child being harmed.

Whenever it was raining on a Saturday or Sunday (so as to foil the devil who was waiting to tempt us into mischief if we were not constantly occupied), Colonel Heath would announce at breakfast that there would be a paper chase after dinner.

We would meet outside the Dining Hall, church or wherever bidden, the cottages representing the 'hares' would set the trail and those cottages who were the 'hounds' were informed. The hares set off a while before the hounds.

The day I recall, Jeannie Lucas and I had gone to the cottage to change into our bathers with our cotton dress over the top. We set off through the paddocks and over stiles, the paddocks were clear of trees and seemed to go on for miles. Jeannie and I had just climbed over a stile when we heard a very loud 'moo'. We clung together and stood absolutely still, we were too scared to go on, but then heard the deep loud laugh of Colonel Heath hidden behind some shrubbery.

Suddenly he was beside me, swept me up with his one arm and slung me up on his shoulder. This was pure delight, I could see the whole world, I held on round his neck and he took Jeannie's hand and away we went to catch up with the others. Even though we were the youngest, we completed the whole of the paper chase with the Colonel picking us up once in a while and giving us a lift on his shoulder.

As I grew older I loved those paper chases and trying desperately to find those hares. We never did, we figured they must have cheated and returned home.

A happy memory is the smell of newly mown hay as we walked across the paddocks. I would stop and breathe deeply, it always reminded me of England and a hidden memory of myself as a young child rolling down a hillside covered in clover, the smell and joy of the roly poly fall.

Flo's mother during her teenage years in Wales

21. SUTTON BENEFACTOR

Sundays consisted of a compulsory church service starting at 11 am and finishing about 12.30 pm. In my early days services were conducted by Colonel Heath in the Dining Hall because there was no church. We had a visiting priest once a month.

An English benefactor, Mr Thomas Wall of Sutton, Surrey, gave £6,000 to build a church. A circular stained glass window was given by the Old Fairbridgians' Association. Architecturally, the church was raved about and brought many a visitor to gaze with amazement.

It had a concrete floor and brick walls, the pews were kept highly polished and I used to slide about on them. We had a hassock on which to kneel, very flat on the cement floor and very small. They were collected up and placed on the end of the seat after each service.

The chancel contained the organ and choir seats. There was a beautiful lectern in the shape of a brass eagle and the pulpit was carved wood. The sanctuary had altar rails, the altar with its brass cross and candlesticks and an altar cloth that someone had embroidered.

Evensong was not compulsory and was only for the older children. One of the punishments I bore was to miss out on this service. I liked church and going without was real punishment. I enjoyed it for two reasons, firstly, the joy of singing hymns and secondly, I felt an affinity with this spiritual life.

The church was called the Church of the Holy Innocents and the

Bishop of Bunbury, our bishop for all important occasions, conducted the service when the foundation stone was laid on 14 February 1931, by Mr Joyner.

Only the boys were chosen for choir singing for in those days, though we girls could clean the chancel, it was considered too Holy for us to sing in the choir on Sundays. The Bishop liked the sound of our British voices and he asked us to practise the Sung Eucharist. I loved this and felt proud to hear him say how much he enjoyed our singing, for we all sang, not just the choir, nearly four hundred children rendering the music with gusto.

Then we had a permanent Padre attached to Fairbridge and he had his own Rectory. From that time he gave all Religious Instruction. We were not considered fit to mix with the Padres' children, whom we referred to as 'private kids'. Canon Watson, an older man, was the only Padre I remember as friendly. He treated us like children, not as gutter children in an institution.

One of the Padres was always reporting kids to their Cottage Mother for small misdemeanours which resulted in punishment when they should have been dismissed as childish pranks and growing up. I remember one episode. All the girls from the cottage and our Cottage Mother were passing the Rectory fence when she instructed one of the girls to pick up some kindling lying on the ground. As she bent to pick it up, the girl said: "Oh, faggit."

The Padre heard her, assumed she swore, and reported this to our Cottage Mother. Embarrassed that one of her girls was being reprimanded by the Padre, our Cottage Mother promised she would be punished. By the time we reached the cottage Miss Kittell remembered that 'faggot' is a term for a bundle of sticks, the girl escaped punishment and off went Miss Kittell to score off that rotten self righteous Padre and regain her pride.

It was strange that I was taught about this God up there who loved me so much he was always rescuing and saving me, but at the same time was spying on me and punishing me. I was so afraid of the God who loved me at Fairbridge that even in my private moments of thought, I would be aware that he was watching me.

It confused my young mind, how could a loving God keep telling tales and reporting me to Authority? I was so awed by this God that in church, while kneeling for those long prayers, if I looked up and glanced in the choir stalls and caught the eye of a particular friend who was a choir singer, I would be racked with guilt thinking what an awful sin I had committed.

This sin would stay with me because I couldn't talk to anyone about my thoughts and for days I could not bring myself to look at Percy, the choir singer, for I felt he knew about my sin.

At the age of eleven it was time for me to be 'prepared for confirmation'. This meant attending regular sessions with the Padre and preparation took months. I had to learn the whole Catechism off by heart along with the Collect from the prayer book, parts of the Bible, three hymns (St Patrick's Breast Plate, Close by the Heedless Workers Side and Come Holy Ghost Our Souls Inspire) and write a composition on what confirmation meant.

I was lucky I had taught myself to memorise poems and I was good at compositions. I ended up telling two cottage girls what to write at the same time as writing my own piece. When the Padre marked them he asked: "Who wrote these compositions?" We all kept quiet so he asked me direct and I was in all honesty able to say that I hadn't written them all, because I had just told the other girls what to write.

The Head Matron was to question me on the Catechism and she did her best to catch me out and send me off to learn it all over again. I also had to recite the Collect to her and my Bible passages. The hymns were recited to the Padre.

Finally, the great day arrived, it was exciting because all us girls were dressed in white with a white veil over our heads. We were scrubbed and polished from head to toe. The boys were neatly dressed in shorts and shirts. The Bishop of Bunbury conducted the service and it had a profound effect on my mind.

I truly felt I had been filled with the gift of the Holy Spirit. If I had been asked to commit my life to the service of the Church, I would have unfalteringly gone ahead and done so. Religion from then was to have a frightening but awe inspiring effect on my life, I found so much beauty in the Church which I was unable to realise, and was to push deep into my subconscious a well of tears of loneliness.

The Church of the Holy Innocents was built on the rise and dominated Fairbridge. You could see it without wanting to. It stood like the head of the table, overseeing all. Yet it never caused me to tremble, it was like a guardian.

The church bell would ring out as a warning of danger, it had a special toll which the adults understood and would quickly assemble at the Principal's house. Sometimes it was a child lost in the hills of the Darling Range and off they would set to look for him. Sometimes the river in flood would be too menacing to ignore. Sometimes it was a fire in the hills and if the risk was great, the senior boys would assist.

I remember jumping out of bed on those nights, especially at the sight of a bushfire, to see the hills alight with thousands of fires and then shivering from the danger – they could have spread to Fairbridge – I would go back to bed and hide under the blankets.

Later, I was to teach Religious Instruction in the day schools of New South Wales – after I did my TH. A (Associate of Theology) which I passed with first class honours – and I could always enthral my young listeners with tales of the church bell that was used for joy as well as danger. Joy was the ringing of the bells for Sunday church.

The bell tower was used by the Colonel. From its top he could oversee much of the school and the orchard, so could spot a thief and also the boys riding on the 'dunny cart' instead of leading the horses. The dunny cart carried the clean and used toilet pans.

He would use the megaphone to sing out: "What do you think you are riding, a chariot? Get down and lead those horses," and we could hear this all over Fairbridge, or so it seemed.

The Church of the Holy Innocents, Fairbridge

22. LEARNING TO BE A LADY

My Cottage Mother wanted more for me than the life she could see me attaining through the Fairbridge system. She wanted to train me to be a 'lady' and to learn the social graces of the day and give me, and other girls in the cottage, a taste for culture, the sort she knew was based on good music, deportment, plays and meeting the right people (her words).

The only way she could have achieved this would be to adopt me or take me out of the system, both of which were impossible. I could never be adopted, this was against the policy of the Child Emigration Society.[8]

Part of her training while I was still a young child was to take me to meet the wealthy landowners, her former employers, when they were back in Perth because the heat was too great for them on their country properties. Miss Kittell would arrange her holidays to coincide with their return to the city and take me to visit for a day. She gave me instructions all the time on how to behave.

I remember the time we were met off the train by a chauffeur driven car and Miss Kittell told me not to open the car door as the chauffeur would do that and not to talk unless spoken to. I was so full of excitement I had to control my natural desire to whoop with joy at this beautiful car, smile happily at the chauffeur and chat away with all my questions. Instead, I stood demurely beside Miss

---

[8] Some children already had parents or guardians, as the London Society told the Dominions Office in 1943. In undated notes Kingsley Fairbridge said he favoured the cottage home system for bringing up destitute children, worried that cheaper options such as boarding out or adoption might lead to their exploitation or their potential not being realised. This is indeed ironic, given later criticism of the farm school.

81

Kittell while he opened the car door and we both stepped in. He placed our luggage in the boot and away we went. Miss Kittell spoke to the chauffeur and told him about me but I just sat back and enjoyed the trip.

We arrived at this big house and I went to open the car door and let myself out when Miss Kittell slapped my hand. The chauffeur opened the door for my Cottage Mother and then came around and opened the door on my side. I stepped out but couldn't say: "Thank you" to him as this was forbidden. It felt all wrong, could a smile really be wrong?

We entered into what was called the waiting room, it was not small and contained a table, wall cupboards, a large grandfather clock and hardback wooden chairs. Miss Kittell was immediately greeted by Mrs Church, the lady of the house, and taken away, I was left to perch on a chair in this room. Everything was so quiet, too quiet, all I could hear was the ticking of the grandfather clock and the striking of the hour, a sound that was to haunt me over the coming years whenever I found myself in the same situation, a feeling of being forgotten.

Miss Kittell must have caught up on all their news for I was left sitting there for well over an hour unable to move (it was forbidden). Miss Kittell then sent me to wash, producing my white pinny, the pretty one inserted with lace, to wear for lunch. I sat down at this beautiful solid table, about four adults and myself, I was introduced and replied correctly with good afternoon.

I was shown how to slide the table napkin out of the silver ring and exactly where to place it on the table. When soup was served, I was shown how to tip the dish to finish the soup and how to place the spoon in the bowl. I was made to get off my chair and carry all the dishes to the servery hatch opening to the kitchen, starting with Mrs Church and going to the left side of her to remove her plate and so on with each person.

I was sent back to the servery to collect the bread board on which was placed a loaf of bread and bread knife. I had to carry this without the knife slipping off and place it in an exact spot on the table. All the time everyone was talking and Miss Kittell keeping an eye on me. Seated again the meal was served, I remember the rockmelon, no sugar allowed. I was told that ladies don't eat sugar on their melon, only salt.

I was also told ladies don't eat sugar on their porridge, only salt, and it finally dawned on me when tea was served that ladies don't take sugar in their tea. There was a finger bowl beside each plate, this was something I had never seen before and it was explained to me that ladies always dipped the tip of their fingers in the bowl and daintily patted them dry on their napkin. I can't say I enjoyed that meal, I liked sugar on rockmelon and porridge.

I was also made to slice the bread at the table. It had to be a certain thickness and then placing the tip of the bread knife into the bread so it would not fall off, I had to hand it to the person whose slice it was. It felt like a real test and that I was being sized up. Once the meal was over, I was left to clean the table and place all the dishes on the servery hatch and then I returned to the waiting room, sitting again on the chair to wait for my Cottage Mother.

These days away with my Cottage Mother were training sessions and as such I have no feeling of delight at all. This contrasts to the days when I was 'out working' and on my holidays my Cottage Mother would take me to the opera. At the place where we were staying we had fish soup for tea, I didn't like it but had been told that ladies ate fish soup and naturally had to force it down.

I think it was going off, for Miss Kittell kept asking me how I felt as she felt quite ill. She told me then never to eat fish soup unless I knew who was making it. I haven't been able to eat it again, I had to take a dose of salts just in case. I learnt it wasn't always right to be a lady.

23. NO BETTER THAN THE REST

Miss Kittell would mock me. "You'll never be a lady" she would say when she was displeased with me over some trifle. When I spoke she would say: "Don't speak in that monotonous voice, you'll never be a lady," when I sang: "Florrie, you have a voice like a mosquito, you'll never be a lady," and often: "Poor Florence, you'll never be a lady," it was rubbed into me morning, noon and night.

I recall the night she was really angry with me, her anger at times seemed out of all proportion and perhaps she felt as frustrated as I did that the situation could not be changed.

My duties at the time were in the kitchen and one job I had was to scrub the long open wooden shelf that sat under the kitchen sink and on which were placed the pots and pans. Everything would be taken off the shelf and with a bucket of warm water, scrubbing brush and Bon Ami brick, the whole shelf would be scrubbed white and when dry all the pans replaced.

It was a fairly difficult job for me being so small, I had the greatest task reaching into the corner and even across the shelf to really scrub hard. All our work was checked before it was passed as finished. Now this job had been performed just the same, the whole day had gone by and I was deep in sleep at about 10 pm.

What had happened I don't know, had Miss Kittell gone to get a saucepan off the shelf or had she suddenly decided to find fault with my work (she used to do this to me and the other girls) and she would look until she could find something to be really cruel about. I was shaken awake and told I was a slovenly girl while being boxed around the ears and pushed roughly.

I was ordered downstairs to do the kitchen shelf. I was slapped again and pushed against the shelf, she told me to bend over and look in the corner at the filth and said: "Filth, like the gutter you came from," and she spat at me saying: "Guttersnipe, clean it."

There was a small ball of fluff in the corner no larger than my thumbnail. With the bucket of water and the Bon Ami and everything off the shelf, I scrubbed it all over again and all the time she was shouting at me: "Guttersnipe, no breeding, no better than the rest."

She spat on the floor, at least not at me again, and she threw every invective she could think of until the job was done. I was shoved roughly out of the kitchen and climbed the stairs to bed. In the morning I had to force myself to remember it hadn't been a dream and that it had really happened. The older girls wanted to know what had happened.

These episodes seared the soul like a branding iron, such were the lengths that some Cottage Mothers[9] would go to to make trouble for us. I almost suspected that bit of fluff had been found elsewhere and placed there.

It may be hard for the reader to imagine that these things happened but the people in charge of us were not trained personnel, to them it was a paid job (though poorly paid) and a deep resentment existed that we British kids were given free board and lodging, education and health care while they struggled financially, with families of their own. They still had to pay and this sentiment was verbally expressed to me by a very angry woman when she and her husband were in charge of a boy trainees' cottage.

---

[9] In a report headed The Farm School which was with the 1943 report to the Dominions Office, the London Society said: "Efforts have been made by London to improve the quality of the Cottage Mothers (at Pinjarra) but it has remained obstinately a problem without solution."

24. COTTAGE MOTHER'S PET

I didn't rise each day thinking life was cruel, hard and bitter, we hoped each day would be good. I lived it according to the timetable set down, I accepted, as the young do, any unexpected joy that came along.

I had a banksia cone, all dry and prickly and to me it looked like a hedgehog, so I tied a string around it and called it Freddy and dragged him with me wherever I went off duty. When we set out on one of our occasional picnics Miss Kittell would carry lollies in her bag and give us all one. I would say: "What about Freddy?" and receive a sweet for him as well.

I was only being a child and never thought of the effect this was having on the other girls, I should not have been favoured but was the only one with an imaginary pet. A lot of the isolation within myself arose because my Cottage Mother took me over as the child she never had and I was not left alone to be one of the mob.

When I was about eight or nine years old one of my jobs was to take Miss Kittell her morning tea and slice of thin bread and butter. This task took about twenty minutes, involving the laying and lighting of the fire in the stove to boil a saucepan of water.

We were not supposed to blow the fire to get it going but I used to blow the baby flame. Another rule was not to leave the ring off the top of the stove and let the saucepan feel the direct flame but I ignored this as it was the only way to get it to boil quickly.

The tray was taken in while the tea was boiling hot to Miss Kittell who was waiting in bed. Nearly always she said: "Get into the bed with me, Florrie, and share some of my tea." She would give me the teaspoon to have a sip and I would stay warm beside her until her tea was finished.

One morning one of the senior girls came in to ask a question and while Miss Kittell was talking I felt mischievous and took a few more sips of the lovely hot sweet tea. When she stopped talking, I was halfway through the cup. She was very angry and pushed me out of bed, telling me what a nasty greedy ungrateful girl I was and never again did I share a cup of tea in bed with her.

I did myself a favour for I did not realise what effect this favouritism was having on some of the girls. I did not learn of this until I returned to Fairbridge aged sixty six, for the first time since leaving Western Australia at twenty one. I was greeted by some of my cottage girls who said: "It was alright for you, Florrie, you were a pet."

I never realised that this was how I was viewed by them and it distressed me. Yet this favouritism was often able to save them all from punishment.

Our whole life at Fairbridge was built on deceit[10] because we were always being accused of lying, stealing, practising sexual acts or encouraging the boys in our thoughts and actions. I believe most of us were completely innocent and normal accidents such as a dripping tap were viewed as deliberate acts of laziness and breaking the rules.

A dripping tap (which probably would never have been noticed in the old stone bath) left a yellow mark in the enamel bath and this was seen by our Cottage Mother. On arrival home from school, we were all gathered in the laundry and asked who had left the tap dripping. I stood there with rest of the girls, it was not usual to use

---

[10] Geoffrey Thomas reported that an 'attitude of trust' in the children was 'not sufficiently in evidence' among cottage mothers.

the bathroom tap except for bathing, normal washing of hands was done in the laundry. Someone might have used the bathroom if the laundry taps were busy. We all stood there as usual waiting for someone to speak.

Now it was not easy to 'own up' to a deed even if there was a culprit, because in addition to a lecture on dripping taps there was punishment. It was always reinforced as a crime committed by an ungrateful child. Our Cottage Mother announced that if no one owned up there would be no pictures that night. She then went to her room and shut the door.

We all started questioning each other about the deed, none of us thought that maybe Miss Kittell had done it and of course we were not told about tap washers needing replacing. I announced that I would say I had done it, I figured our Cottage Mother would let me off and I could go to the pictures, but I needed a plausible story.

The only theme was that I had washed my hands over the bath before school and mustn't have turned the tap off properly. I went over it to ensure there were no flaws. I went to her room and was cross examined: "Why has it taken you so long to own up? Why did you wash your hands? When did you wash your hands? Why did you use the bathroom tap?"

I then received a lecture about what an evil person I was and how she expected so much more from me, and it went on. I wished I hadn't owned up, she left me in her room while she told the other girls they could go to the pictures, I was questioned further and at the last possible moment she let me go. I don't believe she accepted my story but neither could she call me a liar, there was no proof either way.

25. PICNICS

It took us about twenty minutes to walk from Shakespeare Cottage to our special spot in the hills where occasionally we went for picnics. Picnics were occasional because our elderly Cottage Mother found it difficult, not so much the distance but the uneven climb into the hills. Every cottage had its own spot and nobody ever encroached on another's picnic ground.

Our spot was right beside the Darling River, large boulders protruded from the water and we would jump from boulder to boulder. When I visited this spot later when I was eighteen, I realised the danger of slipping between these boulders and knew I could never again jump without fear like I did as a child.

Our Cottage Mother would sit herself as comfortably as possible on a grassy patch while we ran off and enjoyed the freedom, floating boats, boulder jumping, in summer swimming in rock pools. We used to catch 'gilgies' (as they were known in Western Australia) or yabbies, like freshwater lobsters of different sizes, and take them home in a tin where the poor things usually died. Sometimes we gathered the beautiful wild flowers that grew in the hills and always we returned with armfuls of wood for the fire.

Preparation for the picnic involved cooking hundreds of biscuits, ginger nuts, often coconut fingers and sometimes jam kisses. Those we didn't take were stored for future use. I remember one occasion when it was my turn to do the cooking, I was about eleven or twelve years old and was doing this job alone.

The large baking trays were floured and sitting on the table I had a very large bowl in which were the flour, ginger, sugar and other ingredients. The Cottage Mother had walked into the kitchen a number of times to see the preparation was correctly weighed but mainly to see that I was not stealing the mixture by eating it raw. As with all jobs, there was a horrible suspicion hanging over our heads.

Miss Kittell watched as I added the milk to the weighed dry ingredients and mixed them with my very clean hands as this was the easiest way to do it. I got it to the right consistency for rolling when Miss Kittell snapped from behind me: "What have you done with the mixture?"

"Nothing," I replied. "Yes you have, you have been eating it, there should be a lot more mixture," she announced. I looked at her in disbelief and then anger and told her I hadn't eaten any of it and returned to start rolling the mixture. In that instant, Miss Kittell slapped me with such force with the flat of her hand on the top of my spine, one, two, three deliberate belts of cruelty.

I don't recall what happened next but the effect of this on my body and mind was momentous. When I came round I was screaming and banging my hands and stamping my feet. Miss Kittell's face was full of fear, the other girls told me that everybody had gone quiet from fright. I was in such a bad state, somebody had to take over making the biscuits.

I could not bring myself to speak to my Cottage Mother or she to me except with orders for twelve months. Over this period she wrote in my reports that I was not pulling my weight and that I had changed from that sweet pliable person I had been.

In the end, she did talk to me saying it made her unhappy to see me acting this way and lecturing me on setting an example, she thought that I had come from 'better stock'. She expected a lot from me so as to be a credit to her cottage and Fairbridge. Though I tried to be friendly I was never the same as before.

26. PUNISHMENT

Punishment loomed large in our lives, always somewhere in a cottage somebody was being thrashed with a strap on the bare bottom, the BTM as it was described, as if life wasn't punishing enough through deprivation of home, family and country.

The screams of the victims could be heard as you passed a cottage, especially Kitchener Cottage which was a boys' cottage and they had a sadistic Cottage Mother. These boys told me later that they used to start screaming early in the hope of lessening the blows, they had learnt it did not pay to keep quiet as the beatings went on for longer.

To be able to survive the system, you had to be a good student or have a particular gift, acting, writing, singing or sport. If you could not accept the constraints of having to fit into a pattern, you were always in trouble. With the boys this meant continued physical punishment, some girls were thrashed by their Cottage Mothers.[11] Even so, boys had more leeway. Our Headmaster Mr Healey said to us one day: "Boys are allowed to be boys," mischief it was understood being part of them but girls were expected to be models of perfection.

Punishment was given at school for misbehaviour and it was something that worried Mr Healey and the other teachers for on returning to our cottages, if the Cottage Mother found out you were punished at school, she would punish you again.

---

[11] Geoffrey Thomas reported in 1941: "As far as I know the whipping of girls is very fortunately a thing of the past." One cottage mother did not share this relief, however, and several times had been heard to say: "What that girl needs is a good thrashing – a sound whipping would do her a lot of good."

Born: 31st January 1921 at West Derby, Liverpool

Admitted to Barnardo's: 12th January 1926

ACS/PFS/VC

Barnardos

AFTER CARE SECTION

Tanners Lane
Barkingside
Ilford, Essex
IG6 1QG
Telephone 081-550 8822
[Fax 081-551 6870]

5th November 1991

FLORENCE MURIEL BROWN

Born: 31st January 1921 at West Derby, Liverpool

Relatives as at 12th January 1926

Mother:	Ruth Massey nee Fielding Died 8.12.1923
Father:	not known

Mother's first husband:

George Brown, killed in explosion at Pembrey Munition Works, South Wales in 1917

Mother's second husband:

Joseph Samuel Massey (25), Almond Street, Liverpool

Sister: Gwynneth Georgina, born: 19.10.1917 Carmarthen

Half-brother: Joseph Massey (2) at time of admission Joseph in Alder Hey Hospital

Relatives (all maternal):

uncles ⟨handwritten⟩ John Fielding   (46) Garston, Liverpool

∪ aunts ⟨handwritten⟩ Thomas   (44) A carter
                          married, 3 (8) children
                          Fairview Place, Liverpool

              Charles   (38) Window blind maker
                                      married, 2 children
                                      Melville Place, Liverpool

              Joseph   (34) Dock labourer
                                      married, 4 children
                                      Peter Road, Liverpool

              Elizabeth Doughty (20+) Husband a dock labourer
                                       married, 7 children
                                       Wimbledon Street, Liverpool

Flo's family at the time that she and Gwynneth were put into Barnardo's. 'Uncles and aunts' was written in by her. The date of her mother's death here does not match that on her death certificate

92

I remember Mr Healey talking about this and saying that one punishment was enough, but he never managed to stop it. Miss Kittell, though she did use thrashings, was more inclined to slap and box ears and she had a very hard slap which really hurt.

The other horrible punishment was castor oil,[12] but this came to an end after a child died. Next door to Shakespeare was Clive Cottage and one day one of the girls there awoke with abdominal pains and told her Cottage Mother. The Cottage Mother dismissed her, saying (as was her favourite saying): "Bunkum, bunkum, be off, be off."

Now the hospital was only across the road and she could have sent the girl for a check up. Each time the girl went back to her Cottage Mother to report the pain she was given the same reply. On the fourth occasion, the Cottage Mother in anger administered a dose of castor oil.

The child died the next day in the Pinjarra Hospital from peritonitis. From that day our Doctor forbade the giving of castor oil except on his or Sister's authority.

Other punishments would be to deprive us of the enjoyment of dancing, swimming, pictures or, in my case, sport. We would also be sent to bed without our tea, all alone, no lights on, no reading, dry bread or bread and dripping and a glass of water brought to you and no talking to the girl delivering it. I hated isolation but preferred it to physical punishment.

It was not the fear of pain that I hated so much, but the injustice of the whole system and the indignity of the thrashing loomed very large in my mind. Pain, after all, was only momentary and I've learnt to bear that well but injustice sears the soul and indignity

---

[12] The castor oil punishment was adapted by Kingsley Fairbridge from Mussolini, according to Kingsley's wife Ruby, and was based on the effectiveness of ridicule rather than force (Fairbridge Farm, p. 171).

ruins the life. Miss Kittell, when she wanted to show up one of the children, would gather us all round the playroom table and then start accusing someone of a crime of which there was absolutely no proof.

I look back on myself now and wonder how I dared do what I did to protest. I could not cry out: "This is not fair, you are accusing this girl of things she hasn't done." Miss Kittell, telling us of the thrashing she is going to receive, bent her over the tin trunk behind the curtain and belted her with the strap.

I can remember in that whole group of girls standing around the table suddenly turning my back on the whole procedure. It was the only protest I could make and I feel I must have been twelve or thirteen years old at this stage. Not a word was said to me and no action was taken, it was so futile my protesting.

If any girl or boy did clash very badly with their Cottage Mother and was always in trouble with Authority, they would be given an intelligence test and one of the questions they were asked was: "What is today's date?"

Now how often do we have to think of this answer, yet if the child could not reply quickly they were considered to be lacking in intelligence and this was the necessary excuse to send them back to England as 'uncontrollable'. This happened to one of our cottage girls and I often wondered whether she was better off returning to England for she certainly wasn't lacking in intelligence but she was continually in trouble.

Most of the boys were sent to Colonel Heath and he would punish them privately or publicly whenever their Cottage Mother was unable to control them.

27. THRASHING THREATENED

Only once I was threatened with a thrashing and I was then fourteen years of age and training to go 'out to work'. While training, we came under the control of the Head Matron. I detested her and she disliked me and mainly because of my Cottage Mother I escaped a lot of her discipline.

My first job was in the Dining Hall, working with another trainee. The Head Matron laid down the format of how each job should be performed. The whole of the Dining Hall floor was scrubbed each week, we did so many patches a day and these patches still had to be wet when she came to inspect our work.

We had so many windows to clean and the walls to polish, the table tops were scrubbed each day. The servery had to be cleaned and the piano dusted. We all had a day in which to do all of this and it was hard trying to spread out the jobs so that should the Head Matron come in we were still working. As for keeping the patches wet that we had already scrubbed, we would continually wet the floor with a mop until it was examined.

On one particular day we had completed all our jobs and weren't expecting to have our work examined until the usual time around 11.45 am which gave us time to clean up for dinner. I suggested to the other trainee that we try our handsprings (putting our hands on the floor and springing up with our feet against the wall).

It was easy enough to rub off any marks our bare feet made so we tucked our dress and large white apron into the legs of our bloomers and away we went until the Head Matron's voice boomed out: "What are you doing?" Fear descended and I spoke for both of us, explaining that we had finished all our jobs and were practising our handsprings, luckily our patches of scrubbing were still wet.

In an absolute fury, she managed to find fault with all our jobs and turning on me said she would be back after lunch to give me a thrashing. I felt such fear that I had never felt before or since, I was ill with the thought of it and at the same time felt such loathing, hate and anger.

It took over my whole body and I thought, if I get thrashed I will turn so wicked and evil and I shall be bad as I can be good. It was a physical force inside me beginning to swell and take over, I shall never forget the feeling, I had gone pale and turned ill as if with a great sickness.

My Cottage Mother noticed my agitation at lunch and asked me what was wrong. I told her I had been threatened with a thrashing and she asked me the reason. I explained the incident and also told her how difficult it was to spread the work out to fill in the time.

She went and saw Colonel Heath and in the afternoon I was back at work and waiting in fear but instead of the Head Matron, Colonel Heath appeared. He asked me what the trouble was and following my explanation also asked my co worker so we both poured out our problems. I always found Colonel Heath to be fair and after he had listened he patted me on the head, said not to worry and left.

I never got that thrashing but neither did I know that I wasn't going to get it. I suffered all afternoon before I realised the Head Matron wasn't coming. When I returned, my Cottage Mother asked me how I was and then told me she had been to see the Colonel. Actually, the Head Matron had been looking for an excuse to thrash me, such was her dislike for me.

My second job was in the church and meant I had to live in the

Guest House with six other girls and the Head Matron also had her quarters there.

She put us through a sadistic ritual each morning. It was the duty of one girl to fill the bath each evening with water right to the top in preparation for our cold plunge in the morning. It was not sufficient for the Head Matron that we just dip in and out of the water. She sat herself on a chair at the end of the bath, while we stood there naked and, one by one, lined up and standing beside the bath, we would wet the soap and, shiveringly, soap ourselves all over.

This done to her satisfaction, we would plunge into the water, rinse the soap off, then out of the bath to grab a towel while still being observed. I would always race to the septic (tank) toilet and sitting there would let the warm urine leave my body and feel the warmth of it for a few seconds rise to comfort me.

We always had a few days' break from the plunge when we had our periods but to be believed we had to show the soiled pad to the Head Matron and she would make dirty remarks about how many boys did we tell we had our periods. I can't recall discussing my periods with another girl, let alone wanting the boys to know.

How did these sadists[13] get employed to look after us kids, how is it nobody knew?

---

[13] An Old Fairbridgian aged 82 who was at Fairbridge from 1927-31 told Flo in a 1997 letter that a prime fault of the scheme was that it was pure luck whether you drew a motherly type or a sadist. He has always been very bitter about his treatment by a Glasgow Cottage mother and Colonel Heath. "It was child abuse at its worst."

Health care was firstly in the hands of our Cottage Mother. When I was feeling ill, it was very hard to be believed. I don't know what symptom in the end would convince Miss Kittell that I or anyone else was not pretending. I along with most of the other children at Fairbridge kept very well.

I did suffer from headaches and have done nearly all my life. I would report this fact to Miss Kittell and mostly would be sent off to school to get on with it, no medication of any sort unless it was the threat of castor oil (before it was banned unless on Doctor's or Sister's authority), liquorice powder or Epsom salts. Consequently, you bore bodily with discomfort rather than face one of these horrible purgatives.

I remember a flu epidemic that finally hit Fairbridge but precautions had been taken to protect us all. In the first place, Mr Joyner, whom we kids didn't like at all, was hit by the virus. We were told that 2 am was the critical time for the disease with night nurses watching for the crisis to come and go.

We kids went around saying Mr Joyner opened the window and in – flu – enza. We felt secretly pleased and hoped the horrible man would die. He had an arrogant attitude towards us and was always reluctant to approve the purchase of necessary replacement equipment. We were told the disease could come to all of us. We had no realisation of the tremendous responsibility the adults had to face, but for a fortnight our whole life changed.

There was no school, we were not to gather together in large groups, no Dining Hall meals, all our meals would be delivered to our cottages. We had to stay outside in the fresh air as much as possible, only being inside to sleep. Every morning on rising, each one of us was given a very weak solution of Condy's Crystals, an antiseptic, to inhale up each nostril, no swallowing, it was a poisonous substance, and each morning we gargled with this solution.

We lost only one boy and girl before the epidemic passed, I remember being told that both had a weak chest, and how sad it was for us. At the same time, what a marvellous job was done to contain such a potential killer.

Naturally, I felt no sense of danger, it was a glorious fortnight of change, a feeling of release, despite the fact that life went on just the same except in the isolation of our cottage. We could still sing out to the kids in the other cottages near us but what a strain it must have been on our Cottage Mothers and the rest of the Staff.

One Saturday I woke up with terrible abdominal pains. I was not gastric, just doubled up with pain and the only way I could get any relief was to rush to the hard lockers in the sitting room and lie flat on my stomach and not move. I suffered this way nearly all day before my Cottage Mother sent for Sister.

Sister came to our cottage and had, like everyone else, a suspicion that I was 'bunging it on' or pretending. She checked me over just in case of appendicitis and then told Miss Kittell that she was going to keep me in hospital overnight to watch me.

That was the only time I ever went to hospital, I'll never know what caused the pain, I never saw the Doctor though Sister did ring and tell him. The next morning I was sent home. I did quite often suffer from abdominal pains but unless it got unbearable I just went about my business.

I saw the Doctor only once while at Fairbridge, about my back. I found one morning when I went to make my bed that I could not bend over to lift the mattress to tuck in the sheets, my back was full of pain and the only way I could manage was to rest my weight on one hand and push the sheets under with the other hand.

I suffered this way for a few days before reporting to Miss Kittell. Finally, Sister called me to see the Doctor on one of his visits. I can still see this tall man standing there, he never examined me, just asked for my symptoms. He asked whether I could touch my toes, I said yes and demonstrated and he dismissed me.

Now it was not in that position that my back hurt, it was the half bent position and any one of the numerous back sufferers there are would understand this. In those days it was not understood, you were just malingering and that is what he thought. If he had questioned me I would have recalled what had caused my back to give, instead it was later in life when I was an adult trying with another Doctor's help to remember when I could have injured my back.

It happened this way, we kids would play ball games together in our cottage and one of the games we called 'sevens'. We would get in front of the kitchen's brick chimney and hit the ball seven times in different ways until we were out. In front of the brick chimney was a narrow brick drain, with the bricks on either side of the drain set on their edges forming a very sharp cutting line.

I was standing this day in front of the chimney playing when one of the girls suddenly grabbed my legs and pulled them from under me. I landed with such a sharp bang on the edge of the bricks, I remember screaming, so severe was the pain, and my back had been cut through my clothes.

This was to be the cause of my continuous backache and it was not until an x ray showed up an old injury that I was able to trace the problem. Naturally, however much my back played up on me at

Fairbridge, I could not again report it as the Doctor had dismissed it as being OK.

The other injury which most of us barefooted children suffered was what were called 'stone bruises'. They were very painful and the best way to describe them is to say a small blister would form at the base of the foot near the toes and develop into a larger blister travelling all through the toes. The blister would be yellow in colour as if formed with pus under the skin.

The treatment was to soak the foot in as hot as possible salty water. It took a long time for a stone bruise to heal and at night in bed the foot would throb horribly, making it impossible to sleep. No painkiller of any sort would be given, I don't know whether there was any such thing. The foot would be bandaged to help with walking and forming a pad under the foot. If I remember correctly, an old sock was worn.

My other injuries at Fairbridge were from falling while practising racing. Whenever I had to do anything I would run, no one told me to practise, it was my own feeling that I should. One day I ran round the side of the Dining Hall and tripped over a hidden stump and grazed my knees very badly on the rough stony ground.

When I stood up my knees were bleeding and tiny pebbles were stuck in the wound. I was told by an adult not to wash my knees but to sit down quietly and gently brush off the pebbles. It hurt unbelievably and I can't remember if I had any other treatment. If I had it would have been to rub Vaseline into my knees. Vaseline was the treatment for most cuts and bruises.

29. LISP ANNOYED ADULTS

Teeth were checked for cavities. Apparently, the water from the hills that we used was full of a naturally occurring chemical and consequently when I left Fairbridge my teeth started to break down and had to have fillings.[14]

Even when we were working, we were still in the care of Fairbridge until twenty one and had to seek permission to go to the Dentist. Mostly I went to the Fairbridge Dentist in Perth. Fairbridge would pay and then deduct it from my wages.

The dental work I received at Fairbridge attempted to straighten my teeth. My teeth were described as 'overcrowded' and were pushed out of place and one molar in particular was pushed backward into my mouth.

The real reason for the attention to my teeth was that I had a lisp and this annoyed some of the adults and upset my Cottage Mother. Often people would ask me if I was tongue tied. It was decided that a crooked canine tooth must be preventing me from speaking properly and that I would go to Perth for treatment. There were about five of us taken in a car by the farm school driver.

My tooth was straightened by a method known as the regulation plate. This had a spring placed behind the offending tooth which was retightened every fortnight. It did straighten my tooth but also left it very weak and in my forties it finally broke off. When I was wearing this plate it sounded as if I had a lolly in my mouth.

[14] In a note on Geoffrey Thomas's report, London said that there were always some cases of osteomyelitis at Pinjarra, although none at its other farm schools, and wondered whether there was some link with the water supply or excessive swimming in the river.

My Cottage Mother and girls all recognised this but one day Miss Kittell asked me to take a message to another Cottage Mother. I duly knocked on the door and she came to speak to me. I had only just started to deliver the message when she told me in annoyance to take the sweet out of my mouth before speaking to her.

I recall with glee saying so politely: "I haven't got a sweet in my mouth, Miss, I've got a regulation plate." Of course I wasn't believed until I showed her the offending article. I can always remember in my childish way feeling that I had really scored that time, as she wasn't a very nice person and would have had great delight in having me punished for addressing her with a lolly in my mouth.

Marjorie Rick (Rickie), left, and Joan Carter, Flo with a fan, Jeannie Lucas beside her. They had dressed up in sheets waiting to go to the laundry and strolled around Fairbridge. In the background is the Rectory

103

30. MY NAKED BOTTOM HAD BEEN SEEN

Housemaids' knee was a complaint from which I suffered but fortunately not as badly as some of the other girls. This was caused by kneeling and fluid would build up, swelling the knee to twice its size. The only treatment was firm bandaging with a crepe bandage. You couldn't of course kneel for a while to work but this didn't mean that you escaped from jobs, others would be found.

It was very painful and I know some of the girls suffered over and over again from this complaint. As soon as the swelling was down, it was back to kneeling for scrubbing and polishing and no pads on which to kneel, so naturally the cycle continued.

Another job that required the use of knees was cleaning the lavatory. This contained a wooden seat over the pan system and a wooden floor. My job was to scrub the seat and floor with phenyl and water, it smelled good if nothing else and I really scrubbed.

I have two vivid memories of that lavatory. Firstly, I was sitting on the lavatory when to my horror the lid at the back was lifted up and the pan over which I was sitting was removed and replaced with the clean pan. Away went the two boys to place the full pan on the dunny cart while I sat there frozen to the seat.

I was quite sure that they would know who it was, my naked bottom had been seen and they would know it was Florrie Brown.

How could I ever look again at those senior boys. Though I can laugh about it now, the discomfort of that moment stayed with me. I could not speak to anyone of my disgrace, it just sank lower and lower into my being until time hid it, even from me.

The other memory resulted from my fear of cats and dogs fighting, in the same way that some people are afraid of snakes and spiders.

One morning I wanted to go to the lavatory. I went part of the way down the back steps when the most bloodcurdling sound of cats fighting broke the air and the two cats flew under the steps, scratching and clawing and squawking. I was so unprepared for this that I screamed and screamed as I flew to the toilet.

My Cottage Mother and some of the girls rushed out to see what had happened. I sat in that toilet shaking and when I finally got into the cottage, my Cottage Mother was too distressed for me to punish me. Some of the senior girls explained that it was only cats fighting and I did eventually train myself to overcome most fear or pain by learning to bear it.

I learnt early that crying or moaning only added to the agony, it didn't decrease it. In my sixties I had a small skin cancer burnt off my nose and lay there feeling the pain without emotion. The Doctor finally asked whether I was trying to be brave.

Another episode was at the birth of my son in my twenties and it was a breech birth. I was given anaesthetic which made me slightly drunk and my leg being in a stirrup, I suddenly heard the tune of the Blue Danube go through my head and started to swing my leg in time with the tune. I could hear the Doctor and Sisters laughing and the Doctor told me to stop it. I stopped immediately and heard him say: "Where did you learn such discipline?"

Another Doctor when I was in my forties and having a pap (cervical) smear told me I was the coolest customer he had ever had. I replied to him that he didn't have me, he only had my body.

I was not aware until I sought counselling in my sixties that that response would unlock the door to the depth of my suffering.

31. LOST IN THE BUSH

For the Royal Perth Show, apart from the tedious but nerve racking sewing of petticoats and pillowslips, we also competed in the floral arrangements and made posies, buttonholes and sprays.

Now wild flowers were not supposed to be picked within a certain radius of Perth and luckily Fairbridge was just beyond that radius. We would go into our bush and pick a variety of flowers.

There were over sixty different wild orchids, my favourite was the spider orchid. There were also kangaroo paws, smoke bush, hovea (a beautiful deep mauve) and what we called the egg and bacon plant carrying small yellow and brown flowers, and the beautiful blue leschenaultia.

I had a special job as it had been discovered that I had a good colour sense and my task was to make the first posy, picking and matching colours until I was satisfied and then the others would copy, quite often making a better posy than mine. The best ones would be chosen for the show. I did the same with the sprays, created the original and also the sheaf and wreath of flowers.

On one occasion I set off with three other girls from Shakespeare Cottage. There was a rough imaginary boundary which limited our walking distance and we set off on our own, it was not often that we got away without an adult in attendance. I was after as much colour as possible and to see the small orchids meant really looking. The orchids were slender with very fine flowery heads and only just managed to appear through the feathery grasses.

Lots of flowers hid under prickly bushes and we only had our hands to use, no tools of any sort. We could not pick too many and no pulling up by the roots. If sometimes in a hurry I did this dreadful thing, I would hide the offending plant inside a deep prickly bush, yet always I thought that someone will find it and I would be in trouble. For weeks I would suffer.

So engrossed was I walking from bush to bush that it was a while before I realised I didn't know where I was. We were a wee bit scared, not so much because we were lost but because it would mean punishment if we were late back.

I wandered around without finding a clue, if only I knew in which direction lay the river, I could then find my way back. I don't really know what inspired me but as I looked down at the ground, I saw a very narrow trickle mark made by water running to the river. I knew if we followed this it would bring us to the river.

It turned out to be quite a walk before we reached the river where we all picnicked with our Cottage Mother and then it was easy to walk back to the farm school. I had a beautiful armful of wild flowers as did the other girls. When we reached the cottage, the explosion took place, no remarks on our flower collection, just why were we so late.

I explained that we had got lost and of course we were not believed. I had to place the flowers in the laundry sink and we were immediately sent to bed without any tea. We were hungry, cold and tired, no talking was allowed but some girls sneaked up with some dry bread for us.

That evening the girls were putting on a concert. I think Miss Kittell encouraged it to make us feel worse. I tiptoed on to the very small landing at the top of the stairs and by lying on my stomach, I was able to see over the top of the sitting room wall which was built in such a way it had a good opening between it and the ceiling. No wonder everyone shivered through winter.

Miss Kittell knew about this peephole and every now and then would get up to see whether we were using it. As soon as I saw her move very silently, I would scurry back to bed. We took turns to look till after a while, hungry and tired, I finally went to sleep.

There was never a remark passed about our beautiful collection of flowers. The next day I was busy arranging them in colour sequence for our displays. These were happy alone moments for me as I developed my gift for blending colours, mauves and white, yellow and browns, blue and grey. There was always an adult in charge to approve of my final choice.

Whether our efforts won prizes, I can't remember if we were ever told. It was not an individual effort but a Fairbridge effort, my part I remember in the same way I see Fairbridge and the way it impacted on my life, as a duty to carry out. You did not look for or expect praise.

Praise unlike punishment was not something that was meted out to us. I had a very lopsided life built on fear, discipline and silence, to be seen and not heard. I did not confide in another girl for fear that what I said would be reported. There was no adult I could talk to about my sense of injustice and I was not able to write to my sister and tell her about the misery of my life. Even later I could not tell the world, for it was a stigma to have been brought up in an orphanage.

32. DORMITORY MEMORIES

The dormitory holds many memories. One of my early childhood memories was the scream of the whistle before my father died. In the dormitory, I would hear a whistle scream out and sit up in bed and announce that someone had just died. When I was ten years old one of the older girls said to me: "Florrie, that is just the train whistle," and from then I was more at peace with myself.

One night I heard these cats having a real fight and I was terribly frightened and got out of bed and climbed into the bed of the lass next to me. If I had been caught punishment would have been severe, we were not supposed to seek comfort from anyone, but I sneaked back into my bed before daylight. I just needed the protection of another human.

One hot sultry night our windows were wide open and there was no fly wire to keep out the insects. A large beetle flew through the window right on to my bed, its spiky legs getting too close to my hair and causing much distress. Miss Kittell came up to see what all the commotion was about, the beetle didn't worry her and she told us it was God punishing us for something we had done wrong.

As the beetle had landed on my bed it must have been something I had done to anger God and I was being cross examined to tell the truth or God would go on punishing me. What could I think of, what had I done? There was no explanation that the hot night, open windows and electric light may have contributed to the beetle's arrival.

Another night Ruby Fairbridge, widow of Kingsley Fairbridge, came to read to us from a book about her husband's life.

Dr. Barnardo's homes: National Incorporated Association.

STEPNEY, CLAPHAM, CLAPTON, HACKNEY, BLACKHEATH (LONDON, ENGLAND);
having branches in

Bristol, Gloucestershire ; Belfast, Ireland ; Liverpool and Birkdale, Lancashire ; Birmingham, Warwickshire ; Bradford, Harrogate, Hull, Leeds, Middlesbrough and Sheffield, Yorkshire ; Hove, Sussex ; Cardiff, Glamorganshire ; Epsom, Surrey ; Exeter and Plymouth, Devonshire ; Felixstowe, Suffolk ; Gorey, Jersey ; Folkestone, Hawkhurst and Tunbridge Wells, Kent ; Barkingside and Woodford Bridge, Essex ; Hertford, Hertfordshire ; Llandudno, Carnarvonshire ; Newcastle, Northumberland ; Northampton, Northamptonshire ; Washington, Durham : North Elmham, Norfolk ; Portsmouth, Shirley and Southampton, Hampshire ; Parkstone, Dorsetshire ; Toronto, Ontario, Canada ; Sydney, New South Wales, Australia ; Pinjarra, Western Australia ; together with BOARDING-OUT CENTRES in rural homes throughout ENGLAND, in ONTARIO, CANADA, and NEW SOUTH WALES, AUSTRALIA, and WESTERN AUSTRALIA

An Agreement made this _____ day of

_____ One thousand nine hundred and _____

between DR. BARNARDO'S HOMES : NATIONAL INCORPORATED ASSOCIATION, 18 to 26, Stepney Causeway, E.1., in the County of Middlesex, of the one part and

of _____

the _____ of _____
hereinafter called the NEXT FRIEND of the other part.

Whereby it is agreed as follows :

(1) The NEXT FRIEND hereby gives up and hands over the said child to the custody of the MANAGERS of the said PROTESTANT HOMES to be taken care of maintained and educated in any one of the Branches named at the head of this Agreement or to be BOARDED-OUT by the aforesaid MANAGERS in the United Kingdom or Canada or Australia as the MANAGERS shall decide.

(2) The NEXT FRIEND agrees that the said child shall be under the Guardianship of the MANAGERS until the said child shall attain the age of twenty-one years or for a shorter period if the MANAGERS think fit and that during the whole term of the said child's residence in the said Homes or Branches the said child shall be brought up in the PROTESTANT FAITH.

(3) The NEXT FRIEND hereby gives consent to the said child being transferred to Canada or Australia if the MANAGERS think desirable at any time not earlier than TWO MONTHS after the said child's admission to the Homes and without further notice being given to the NEXT FRIEND.

(4) The MANAGERS on their part undertake to properly maintain educate and train the said child or cause the said child to be suitably boarded-out in the United Kingdom or Canada or Australia so long as the said child shall remain in their custody.

(5) The NEXT FRIEND shall receive back the said child into h care in case the MANAGERS of the said Homes for the time being shall for any good cause require the said child to be removed from the said Homes.

(6) The NEXT FRIEND shall not before the expiration of the period mentioned in the second Clause of this Agreement remove the said child from the care of the MANAGERS without having first obtained the consent of the MANAGERS for the time being and in case the NEXT FRIEND shall before the expiration of the said term remove the said child with the consent of the MANAGERS the NEXT FRIEND shall previously to such removal repay to the MANAGERS as and for the expense of the maintenance and education of the said child the sum of six shillings for every week during which the said child has resided in any of the said Homes or Branches or been boarded-out as aforesaid together with the cost incurred (if any) for the travelling expenses of the said child to and from the aforesaid Homes or Branches or Boarding-out Centres.

(7) The NEXT FRIEND also gives willing consent to the said MANAGERS to send the said child at any time they may think proper to any person's care or home or situation or place of employment which may be provided for the said child other than at the above-named BRANCHES whether at home or abroad whether in the UNITED KINGDOM or on the CONTINENTS of EUROPE or AMERICA or in ANY of HIS MAJESTY'S COLONIES or DEPENDENCIES.

AS WITNESS

Signature and Address of NEXT FRIEND.

Signature and Address of person representing and acting on behalf of the ASSOCIATION.

Signatures and Addresses of TWO WITNESSES *to* NEXT FRIEND'S *Signature.*

10 9 24

A Barnardo's agreement to take a child. This may have been for young Joe; his father was thought to have intended putting him into Barnardo's as well as Flo and Gwynneth. One of the branches is said to be in Pinjarra, Western Australia, indicating that Fairbridge Farm School was looked on at the time as a Barnardo's branch

I was listening attentively until she said that her husband had rescued us from the gutters of England to give us a new life in Australia and that we were all gutter urchins.[15] I was so angry at her statement I switched off from the story. From that day I hated Ruby Fairbridge.

I have some better memories of the dormitory, particularly learning Christmas carols. Every Christmas we would learn by heart another carol. We were always told there would be no Christmas presents unless we did. I enjoyed learning carols and knew so many that later I filled many a lonely moment singing these carols to myself while walking across paddocks, ironing or cooking when completely alone.

---

[15] Geoffrey Thomas said that more than once in a Sunday sermon 'Canon Burns has told the children that they are lucky to be in Australia (which is true) and no longer in the wretched hovels and slums of the English industrial towns etc. etc'. In The Farm School report, London said of Canon Burns' preaching: "The policy of the London Society has always been to ease the children in regard to any unfortunate family history. . . . Such reminders are . . . a tragic breach of faith on our part that such treatment is possible."

33. PUBERTY

I recall the first signs of puberty, the morning I woke up and had started my periods and had no idea what had happened. I remember the date, 19 September 1932, for I was always being asked the date of my periods. I was eleven years of age.

Although a number of senior girls were having periods I was completely innocent of the fact. No one was allowed to discuss this bodily function, not even between ourselves, it was taboo. I went to my Cottage Mother and told her I had blood in my pyjamas and she said I must have scratched a mosquito bite.

There was no examination of the soiled item, just a dismissal. I went off to school but I was worried. I was getting more and more uncomfortable and sat still all day, I didn't run or play and barely spoke to anyone. I would not even go to the toilet because I was afraid of what was happening and didn't know if I could do myself damage.

At last that long day came to an end and I once more went to see my Cottage Mother and tell her I was still bleeding. This time she believed me but, as was the practice in those days, no explanation was given. I was taken to her room and from behind her cupboard curtain she gave me five large sanitary towels and two safety pins. I was told that I would now be 'unwell' every month on the same date and I was to wear one towel a day. It was like a child's large nappy made of thick towelling and folded in an oblong shape.

It is hard to imagine, all day and all night with the one towel and the stench on a hot day. I was told to pin the towel to the back and front of my bloomers (we also had a belt thing for pinning the sanitary towel to) and the safety pins always made a bulge and I thought everyone knew my shame.

Each morning, I was to find a bucket kept in the long black cupboard under the stairs and soak my towel in the bucket and every evening remove it without anyone seeing me and empty the contents. I would always try to sneak my bucket outside.

I then hand washed the towel. We were never taught about salt removing bloodstains so it was back to the laundry trough to rub and rub with soap and water till not one mark remained on that snow white towel. Then with two pegs I hung it square on the line.

I was to suffer this routine for three years and still I never spoke to any other girl going through the same thing. Even if they had their period at the same time, all I would be aware of was another smelly bucket under the stairs. The girls who as yet knew nothing of periods complained about the smell. The door to the cupboard was kept shut and was out of bounds except for girls with periods.

From then on, my periods were to make such a difference to my life, running was impaired at those times and so too was hockey. My Sports Masters and Sports Mistresses always expected me to be on top form and there were times when I couldn't play well.

As the blood dried on the sanitary cloth it went hard and scraped the inside of my legs and chafed. It was impossible to run. Miss Phillips would roar at the top of her voice: "Florrie Brown, don't you think you are in this match? Start playing or I'll drop you from the team." I felt wretched. I couldn't sing out that I had my period.

There was no swimming, no bathing, no washing of hair. Of course the boys guessed and I remember begging one of them not to throw me in the water and I would be teased unmercifully. Boys always seemed to find out what we couldn't learn or understand about our bodies.

113

34. HOLIDAYS AT MANDURAH

Every year for holidays we would go to Mandurah, about sixteen miles from Fairbridge. Mandurah was on the coast, a great place, and we enjoyed our fortnight's holiday. This was the type of occasion when remembering the date of your period was important as it was frowned on if it started while at camp. It was not accepted that in those early years of puberty periods were not always regular.

I used to get so excited about Mandurah that it was almost impossible to eat breakfast. I was always pleased to have a break from my Cottage Mother for at camp we were in the charge of Colonel Heath, a nursing Sister, the Sports Master for swimming and whoever did the cooking.

We would pile into the Fairbridge bus and I remember on one occasion a boy had an accident when he fiddled with the spare tyre. The valve flew off and took the top off his finger, there was a great commotion for a while until he was taken off the bus.

We would sing, laugh and talk at the tops of our voices all the way. On arrival, if we were in the first batch our first task was to assemble the tents, eight girls or boys to a tent. Our tents were made of heavy canvas with a centre pole and were always erected under supervision, the tent pegs and guy ropes all checked.

We then filled our palliasses which were large hessian bags filled with straw. These beds would be great for the first few nights but then would flatten to be so thin it was like lying on the ground.

Six am was our first dip of the day and this was compulsory. I

114

would run down to the ocean and stare for a while at the edge before plunging in. The initial catching of breath was great, but we were given no time for swimming. It was a quick cold plunge and then back to get dressed and breakfast. It was the Sports Master's job to see everybody entered the water. For some it was real agony.

After breakfast our tents were inspected. All palliasses were taken outside, water was sprinkled on the floor of the tent and it was raked neatly to settle the dust, tent flaps were rolled up. The surroundings were raked for any bits and pieces that might be on the ground and left clean.

We were then free but to stay within camp bounds. The next swim was at 11 am and this was also compulsory, another at 2 pm, then at 4 pm, these were not compulsory but the final one at 6 pm was.

There was a medical tent and one year I developed a sty on my eye. I was standing while the Sister put drops in my eye and then the next thing I was flat on my back. I was prone to fainting and the Sister got such a fright she made me stay most of the day in the hospital tent.

I missed a period one month, my relieving Cottage Mother thought that swimming the month before when my period had not quite finished may have been the cause. When questioned about the date of my period before Mandurah I didn't tell of the missed one.

For reasons unknown to me at the time, a missed period resulted in frightening cross questioning. My period started at camp and on reporting this to Sister, I was accused of lying about the dates, it was like committing a crime. I was threatened with being sent back to Fairbridge so I told her the truth and she said that swimming in salt water had started my period again. I was allowed to stay but there was no swimming for five days and I had to go to her for disposable towels.

115

Following tent inspection, there was sand and clay modelling and a prize was awarded for the best model. This activity was compulsory, clay was obtained from the side of Mandurah estuary. While I was hopeless at modelling, one of the senior boys did a terrific model of Colonel Heath's head, a side view. Underneath it he had formed the words 'Colonel Bonk' (the nickname was because the Colonel was bald).

He probably meant to scrap the words before inspection but with every child admiring the model the inevitable happened, the Colonel strolled around before judging time. He looked but did not say a word. The model should have won the competition, it was usually 3d or 6d and highly prized.

Instead Colonel Heath gathered us around the model and lectured us on disrespect, the boy's punishment was to be confined to barracks for the rest of the day. Except for the compulsory swims, that meant no walking to the village or spending his pocket money, jobs would be found for him and he also missed out on the prize.

After the 11 am swim, it was back to get changed and into the big marquee for our meal. We all had our own tables and would scurry to our place, standing to await the arrival of the Colonel. Notices would be given, followed by grace and then we would sit down and eat.

A particular meal I remember. Bowls of soup were already set out on the table and the smell of the soup had attracted the flies and there they were floating dead on top of the soup. A number of kids were making uncharitable remarks and growling, I just wanted to quickly lift mine out before they did further damage.

The Colonel chastised us on the grumbling, remarking that one lad had claimed his soup contained six non swimmers. Naturally we all laughed and scooped the dead flies out. There must have been at least six non swimmers in all our bowls.

116

We rested for about an hour afterwards before the most exciting time of the day, to go alone to the village and spend the pocket money we had earned for chores performed at camp or money we had earned during the year. I could buy a halfpenny stick, a long gluey sweet you could suck for hours, or a bag of sweets for 3d to be savoured for the rest of the day.

The treat of treats was to go to the open air pictures for 3d and even sit on the seats, up front of course for this price. How my neck ached gazing up so high. It was much more exciting than the picture shows in the Dining Hall because it was a proper theatre and we were on holiday. Sometimes we got into the pictures for nothing but then the proprietor only let us sit on the grass right in front of the screen.

It was the days of the silent film when the pianist provided all the soundtrack. The talkies were beginning to come in but it was a while before we saw them. After the pictures, it was back to the camp for tea and the evening dip. We were not allowed to enter the water until half an hour after eating. This was drummed into us and never in future years could I bring myself to break the habit.

We used to have camp fires and sing along, with lights out by 8 pm, as long as we spoke softly we could chat on for a while. The temperatures at night would often drop and my palliasse had by this time flattened to a thin mat and with only a couple of thin grey blankets I found it difficult to get warm. I would lie flat on my stomach, get as warm as I could and keep very still.

I remember the night of the big storm when so many tents collapsed. I was in a heavy sleep and not aware of the danger until the great commotion. Adults were asking us whether we were all right and checking that our tents were firm and secure and no rain was coming in.

By this time we were wide awake but snug and feeling the tension of the moment. We had to share the tent with eight other girls who were shivering from the cold night air, wrapped in blankets and carrying whatever bedding they could squeeze into our tent. It was a squash but none of us minded and I felt a lot warmer.

The girls said their tent had blown down, luckily nobody had been hurt. Other tents had flooded as well. It seemed a lot of the boys' tents had suffered this fate. Some children got very wet so lots of tents had doubled up accommodation. We were very excited and were chatting away until an adult appeared and ordered us to be q'iet, sleep as best we could and no complaining.

The storm must have passed over quickly after leaving a trail of damage. What a great day we had talking and hearing of the injuries and near misses, probably well exaggerated and much questioning as to whether the tents had been securely erected.

A group of us older girls and boys, all considered strong swimmers, would be given permission to swim across the estuary. I don't know how far it was, I only know it took a long time to swim. Across the middle of the estuary was a sandbank where we would rest before the swim to the other bank where the water was deep.

If I became tired I would float on my back and then go on. We would rest on a hill on the other side of the bank and do the journey back the same way. As a parent, I could never have let my children do this alone without adult supervision, I could have foreseen accidents that could happen. It certainly was survival of the fittest because survive is what you had to do. If you undertook to do a job, you completed it and if you got hurt or anything went wrong, there was punishment to face.

If I was ever asked what was the most embarrassing moment of my life, I would have to say that it happened on one of these swims. My woollen bathers when wet clung to my body. This particular day, I had swum with the group to the other side and was sitting on the bank catching my breath and laughing with the others when suddenly one of the boys very gently with the tip of his finger touched me on my developing breast. Little rosebuds, he said. In one wild moment and without thinking I dived off the bank and rapidly started to swim away.

I couldn't look at that boy for ages afterwards but I have a gentle smile about it now. The boys were able to have free thoughts while as a female we were always accused of 'leading the boys on', whatever this meant. So I grew up with this deep sense of guilt not only in natural sex but everything I did and thought.

I always loved camping at Mandurah. We were known by the Mandurah residents as the Fairbridge kids and I don't remember ever making friends with a 'private' child. We were something of a curiosity, British children with a strange way of speaking, pommies nobody wanted except to populate this large continent. So we kept to ourselves, restrictions and all, and made whatever fun we could together.

If we were in the first batch to go to camp, on leaving we had to tidy the site, leave the tents standing, pack our gear, a last swim, dinner and away to Fairbridge, with the second batch arriving in the afternoon.

If we were in the second batch, it meant helping to pull down the tents and pack up everything ready for next year into the Fairbridge bus. The bus that took us to and from camp was not the one used for going to sports matches, that was much smaller.

This was a big Army type bus which rattled and banged, the seats were along the side with the equipment in the middle. Our luggage was carried in kit bags, one per person, and I think these were held on shelves above our heads.

35. SPECIAL FRIEND

Girls and boys were not allowed to sit together in the Dining Hall at functions so the girls were up one side of the room and the boys, divided by the aisle, on the other side. If any of us had a favourite of the opposite sex, we would sit one on either side of the aisle and smile shyly at each other when nobody was looking.

I've heard since that the boys used to have bets on who was going to get me and I went ahead and chose my own friend. They couldn't get over me choosing Percy Clayson. I can't even recall his face now or which cottage he lived in.

One night there was a special do on and I was excited about going, I was upstairs in the dormitory standing on the balcony when one of the boys from Percy's cottage went by. I sang out to him asking him whether Percy was going to the function. The answer was yes and I knew that Percy would be on the end of the aisle waiting for me with a spare seat on the other side.

I hadn't reckoned on my Cottage Mother overhearing until she walked majestically into the dormitory and boxed me hard across the ears, calling me a horrible wicked bad child and making me undress and go to bed. She made me feel cheap and horrible. It was so bad in her eyes she threatened me with the strap.

She took my clothes and went downstairs. I lay in bed suffering from shock and fear, not knowing what was going to happen. I cried quietly to myself. After everyone had gone, Miss Kittell returned and again told me what a wicked horrible person I was, how I hated these lectures. After I had been in bed for about half an hour she again returned and in harsh tones told me to get dressed as she wanted to go to the show and I would have to sit next to her. I dressed quickly and without saying a word.

We walked in silence to the Dining Hall and the whole place was full. Miss Kittell sat on one side of the aisle and I sat opposite her. Percy on the other end of the aisle gave me a grin but I couldn't look at anyone, I felt from the Colonel down that everyone knew of my sin.

I never made that mistake again and learnt to write notes instead, using a trustworthy friend to hand them over. My Cottage Mother for months after would keep reminding me of my crime and that was how punishment went on. I was expected to be an example, not a normal child doing normal developing things.

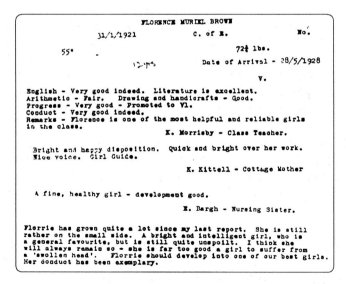

One of Flo's Fairbridge reports, on which she notes that she was 12 years old. The final paragraph was written by the Principal

121

36. GUIDING

When I left England I arrived as a Brownie, I was a pixie and wore my Brownie badge with pride.

As I grew older I stepped into Guides where later I became a patrol leader in the Kookaburra Patrol. I liked being a Girl Guide (or as the non Guides would say, G.G. stands for giddy gubgub) and did the normal Guiding things like passing badges such as swimming. Guiding was a release from the continuous discipline.

Some of the Guides were chosen to go Guiding with other companies and though I can't recall the name of the place, I remember the song we sang around the camp fire:

We are camping down at West Murray
and we're as happy as can be
we came by train and by charrie (charabanc)
to our holiday camp to be
we'll swim and we'll run
we'll work and have some fun
and all the time we are so merry
at our holiday camp we are singing
with the Southern Cross on high.

We would sing this song every night and listen to yarns and tell some ourselves. Everything was well organised but unfortunately we stayed in our own patrols and competed for marks against each other, so in no way were we assimilated.

It was here at camp that I learnt my camping skills and did have fun as well as work. A timetable was placed on the wall in the mess tent and we knew when it was our turn for cooking duty and any of the other jobs we had to perform. What fun and what calamity it was the day the Kookaburras had to cook. None of us had any formal cooking lessons but because we were Guides we were expected to think and work things out for ourselves.

The menu for the day was soup, cold meat and salad, and jelly. We would sing all day long: "Soup, soup, glorious soup." It wasn't really a popular dish however. The Guide Captain produced all the ingredients, vegetables for the soup, lettuce and fruit for the salad, jelly crystals for dessert.

I was the patrol leader and in charge of activities. I had a brainwave and instead of adding salt to the soup I suggested we used seawater and add the chopped vegetables to it. Nobody challenged my idea so we went ahead.

The soup was nicely bubbling away on the camp stove when the Captain in charge of mess duties came in and tasted the soup. "Ugh," she said, then asked us how much salt we had used as it was inedible. I told her what I had done and she didn't growl at me, so I wondered if she really wanted to laugh while she was explaining not to use seawater. We started all over again with the soup.

I had never seen anyone make a salad. I had been told that you washed the lettuce, shredded it and placed it in a tea towel and shook it. I also had to add the sliced oranges and apples in layers.

I carefully laid the tea towel on the table and arranged the shredded lettuce, layers of orange, more layers of apple and more lettuce. I then picked the whole thing up and shook it. I didn't understand why I had to shake it after arranging it so carefully.

Again the Guide Captain had to explain the right technique and the patrol had to rearrange the beautiful creation into salad bowls. Not surprisingly, the jelly didn't set in time. I never knew about using less water and preparing the jelly first so it could be put in the cooler.

There were no refrigerators at camp or ice chests, just the Koolgardie safe. This was made of wire mesh with the shelf on top kept full of water, and cloths that dripped the water slowly down the hessian sides of the safe which was hung or placed in the shade. It really did keep milk fresh and butter firm.

To be successful the jelly should have been made overnight and I as patrol leader should have noted this. The dessert was easily remedied, stewed fruit and custard instead. Needless to say we didn't score high marks for our cooking but I have never forgotten the lessons.

We used to go canoeing and once having learnt to sit in the canoe without tipping myself out, it was great fun. I can still see us all there on the river, giggling as girls fell out of the canoes and some trying to correct themselves by grabbing the canoe nearest them and tipping out that girl as well. Some Guides were never allowed to go canoeing as they were too dangerous to themselves and others.

Those of us who had mastered the art competed in canoe races. I loved this and won as many times as I lost. I also learnt to row a boat and loved the feeling of dipping the oar in the water and the smooth speed of the ride. I was really good at rowing and was given the job of rowing the Guide Captain in charge of the camp whenever she needed to go on the river.

I learnt to fish which was also the subject of patrol competitions. The Kookaburras were neck and neck with another patrol and we needed to catch five fish that day to win. We had a time limit. I rowed our boat and we kept casting out our lines with very little success.

The other boat was close by just in case we found a good spot. Time was running out and we only had two fish when suddenly I came to a deepish hole, which looked black, and I cast my line into it. In no time I had caught a fish, it was very exciting and we didn't leave the hole until we had our winning catch of five fish.

Another exciting fishing trip was done at night in a motor boat. This was owned by a man I assume was a friend of the Guiders. He had taken us out to show us the river in one of its rare moods, it was full of phosphorescence. He stopped the boat and all was quiet when our Guide Captain shone her torch on the water. The unbelievable happened when suddenly fish jumped out and some landed in the boat.

As they broke the water it sparkled like a million silver lights. It seemed the boat was full of fish, the easiest way to fish I knew of. The boat was restarted and we were taken to the pier. There we sat again to watch the water as it hit the pier and broke into all those lights. I have never been lucky enough to see this sight again and I won't forget the thrill of that encounter, nor the fact that I was one of the lucky Guides taken to see it.

I never did this camp again and I don't know whether it was held again. I can still remember all those songs we sang around the camp fires, those lovely fires that shone so warm and bright, always competitions, even in our singing.

Years later, I was to become a Guide Captain myself but Guiding had changed and the silly rules and regulations regarding dress etc nearly killed the movement.

The Duke of Gloucester came to Fairbridge in 1934 and another Guide and I were given the task of opening a fly screen door for him to pass through. It was a double door and required one Guide on each side. We had been practising opening this door together and the hinges had been well oiled to do away with any squeaking.

I was quite excited standing there at the Principal's house, dressed in Guide uniform, and looking forward to meeting the Duke. The moment arrived, absolutely still we were, no smiles on our faces now, we stepped forward to swing back the doors and he stepped through.

He didn't even look at us, nor say: "Thank you," he didn't acknowledge us in any way. I was horrified as I had been taught to smile and say: "Thank you," to be grateful for anything done for me. Nobody had taught me about protocol, that people of high standing didn't even see people like us.

I never got over the fact that his manners were so bad that he had not said: "Thank you." All I could tell the other girls, who excitedly asked for details, was that I didn't like him because he didn't say: "Thank you."

Another visitor, in 1931, was Lord Baden-Powell, founder of the Scouting movement, and I was one of the Guides detailed to show him all over Fairbridge. I proudly showed him the flag I had embroidered for the Kookaburra Patrol. I don't know who had sketched the beautiful kookaburra on the white cloth but I had carefully filled the whole pattern like a tapestry using stem stitch in blues, greys and browns.

38. TRAINING TO BE A DOMESTIC

We left school at fourteen. I actually left at thirteen because of the finishing of the school year and I was to start training to Go out into the World at Middlemore Cottage, where we were given instruction on jobs.

The jobs which we did as training for domestic farm work were in the Dining Hall, the church, the Principal's house, the Guest House, the laundry and in private homes such as the Rectory, the Headmaster's house, the Engineer's house and the hospital.

I was expected to have three months' training at any four of these jobs, give or take a week or two, and when considered 'good enough' was sent 'out to work'. I would be paid 3d or 6d for a month's work, depending on the trainer's assessment. I never was paid 6d.

My first job, as I have already said, was in the Dining Hall. One time I got mid morning tea out of the drawer in the servery, it was usually bread and dripping or bread and jam sandwich, and there eating my sandwich was a fat grey mouse. I grabbed the mouse by the tail and pulled it out of the drawer, it was swinging back and forth and nipped me on the finger, a double insult. I killed that poor mouse mostly because it had the cheek to nip me.

There was a special uniform for all female trainees. Over a ticking type frock you wore a large white apron, it was like another frock over the top and I had to wear a cap on my head. Both apron and cap were like nurses used to wear. I hated the cap as my head would get hot and sweaty and my hair appeared to thin out from being continually covered.

127

It was forbidden to remove the apron or push the cap off the forehead to the back of the head. I think the whole idea of the Head Matron, who set these rules, was to make us look as ugly as possible, it would have suited her ugly mind.

The apron was so massive it had to be tucked up to work. You can imagine, when scrubbing the floor on hands and knees, it would drag through the grey water and hang all wet and uncomfortable against your legs. I was forbidden to tuck in the apron, but I and everyone else did it and hoped not to get caught.

I would grab the corners of the apron and tuck them into the band at the waist on the side where the top of the apron was shaped like a bib. Some of the girls would tuck dress and apron into the leg of their bloomers but it wasn't worth the beating if you got caught.

I was in the Dining Hall training for about three months. My next job, cleaning the church, was very lonely and spooky, because churches to the young often evoke fear and mystery.

I had also been taught about a God who was forever watching me and who knew all my thoughts and whether I scratched myself or picked my nose and other forbidden habits. This caused me great embarrassment to know God had seen me doing these evil things. So there I was in his house with all his angels and spirits around and who knows what voices I might hear in that eerie stillness.

After rising at 5.30 am, dressed except for my bare feet, my job was to weed around the trees outside the Guest House. There was heavy frost and I was frozen. I used to try and stamp my feet up and down to bring life back to them but the stones were too painful underfoot.

After breakfast, my job started in the church. I commenced by beating every hassock together, two by two. I would walk out of one church door into the open, then bang bang and back through the other church door, replacing the hassocks on the seats. Over four hundred hassocks were beaten this way every week.

Again there was a ritual whereby so much of the church cement floor was scrubbed each day and still had to be wet when inspected. All scrubbing on hands and knees. It took the whole week for this cleaning, but then the altar rails and all the brass ware from off the altar had to be cleaned. I was not Holy enough to remove the cross and candlesticks and had to remind the Head Matron every Friday to come and remove them for me.

If I forgot to do this early in the morning, she would deliberately forget too and then would tell me I would not receive my 3d for the month. The brass ware would be taken to the laundry in the Guest House where I was required to clean it. When done, it was inspected by the Head Matron who covered up the Holy relics and carried them back and placed them on the altar.

The same things happened cleaning the church as in the Dining Hall, if the Head Matron was late for inspection and the scrubbed floor was dry, I was accused of not doing it and would have to redo it for further inspection. Also so many pews were to be polished each day and you never made the mistake of pronouncing you had polished more for then the whole job was condemned as 'slipshod' and had to be done all over again.

A lot of my time was spent just sitting on a pew to fill in the time, becoming more and more afraid in the eerie silence. Thank goodness for the noise of footsteps on the gravel path which gave a warning of the Head Matron's approach.

One week, our Padre preaching from the pulpit told us how St Paul's Cathedral in London needed repairing and they were looking for funds from all over the world. I remember saying to God: "If I had two shillings I would give it to you." Some weeks later while I was cleaning the church visitors from overseas came

129

to look at its architecture and I enjoyed pointing out what I knew of the unusual window shaping, the beautiful font with its silver bowl and, as the visitors were about to leave, one of the men put out his hand to shake mine and say: "Thank you."

I enjoyed having my hand shaken in appreciation, it had never been done before and as I brought my palm away, he had managed to wedge two shillings in my hand. Emotions flooded over me, firstly, shame that I had been tipped for doing my job and something I enjoyed doing. I wanted to run and give it back to them, somehow I didn't feel clean, yet I knew I could not do this.

I sat in the pew looking at the two shillings, then I had to hide it before the Head Matron saw it for she would have accused me of stealing it from somewhere. I then remembered my promise to God but it took me three weeks to put that two shillings in the collection plate. I had great tussles with my conscience but I could not rest and, to make matters worse, nobody knew of my great sacrifice and giving it up really hurt. I have never forgotten that two shillings.

The Anglican Church had such an influence on my life, I had a need to serve the Church but I was never able to develop this till I was married, then I ran Sunday schools and taught in them, sang in choirs, gave addresses from the pulpit on occasions such as Mothers' Day and addressed many Church groups such as the Mothers' Union.

It was then that Christianity became all pain to me. There was more lip service than real help, it didn't practise what it preached, especially when I needed help when my marriage was very difficult. It gave me a great guilt complex about my life.

There was another sacrifice in giving up earnings I had no choice in making. We had a plague of mice in Shakespeare Cottage and our Cottage Mother said she would give a penny for every mouse caught. I had a knack of setting mousetraps and I caught fourteen mice, she gave me a penny each time and it was put in the tin behind her curtain but I knew how much I had earned.

Along came Lent, that time in the Church calendar when a person has to give up something, it was a deadly dull time of long faces and no joys. I had nothing to give up but Miss Kittell remembered the fourteen pence. That really hurt for, like the two shillings, I earned that using my own skill. Strangely enough, all my life Lent is a time of personal sorrow. No wonder it was to be back in that church that finally the dam would break.

Flo as a teenager in Perth

39. JUDGE NOT

My next job was in the laundry with the Head Matron's married daughter in charge. I never really got to know her or the job as I was only there for a month because I was too short to reach the troughs, ironing presses or anything else with safety. She reported this to the Head Matron and was very annoyed when I was moved. She and the Head Matron would often fight over us girls.

The next session was at the Guest House from where I worked in the Principal's house. Miss Kittell rescued me from living at the Guest House and the sadistic Head Matron. She must have questioned me for I never ran to her with any complaints or thought of doing so. She told Colonel Heath that she wanted me back in Shakespeare Cottage. I would dress each morning in my trainee uniform and after breakfast report to the Head Matron. Of course I did not realise how lucky I was, and to be called in to work in the Principal's house was considered a very trustworthy job.

But I lived in fear of it, having listened to the stories of the other girls who had worked there and hated it. They warned me never to be quiet while working or you would be accused of going through their drawers and jewellery or sneaking around the place. I was told to bang the bucket on the floor and to hit the broom against the boards, making regular noise like when I cleaned the Headmaster's classroom.

There was a fairly large balcony that had to be done with sump oil and kerosene, a hands and knees job, still wearing that large white apron, still forbidden to tuck it up, but of course I had to or have it covered by sump oil. Mrs Heath used to come up silently to try to catch me out.

Part of my duties was to serve out the milk to all the cottages each morning and night. I would have a large urn of milk delivered to the Guest House, the children would arrive with large enamel jugs and I was told how many pints each cottage wanted. I had a two pint measure and a one pint measure to dip into the urn.

I rather liked this job as it enabled me to have a laugh and joke with the kids. Every second Sunday I was given relief from this task and one Sunday forgot I was on duty. I was given a dressing down and punished by having to learn the Collect for the day.

Sometimes those Collects were not easy to memorise, especially ones on fornication of which I had no understanding. I was also made to learn a passage from the Bible and by lunchtime I knew both pieces. I can't remember the Collect but I have never forgotten the Bible passage: "Judge not that thou be not judged. For whom so ever you judge, so shall yourself be judged," etc.

It was a difficult piece to learn by memory but, as I quoted it to the Head Matron, my whole being was saying how dare you judge me or us kids, await your turn. I can still feel the anger as I write and she was really mad that I had been able to get my tongue around and memorise all those 'judges'.

I had done a total of nine months' training and had learnt nothing but how to clean. Some of the girls were lucky enough to work in the private homes at the farm school and were at least taught some cooking different from the bulk deep fry cooking we did in the cottages.

I was considered a 'credit to the school' and instead of doing another three months' training I was to go 'out to work'. Prospective employers wrote to Fairbridge seeking girls, and correspondence back and forth would take place.

I was fitted out with two pairs of bloomers, two singlets (one on and one in the wash), a warm flannelette petticoat, work dresses of a darker colour cotton and one good dress in a pretty print, shoes, stockings, hankies, toiletries, pyjamas, two pair large sanitary pads and a hat for church.

They were mostly clothes that girls had brought from England, and had been put away for just this reason, but we used to make the odd dress ready to take with us. I made a check dress all by hand and was very proud of this.

Sturdy walking shoes were also in the storeroom, how my feet suffered after all those years of bare feet. Our cases were also ones that had come all the way from England with us.

The other requirement was to attend a lecture with Sister on the facts of life and I had to arrange this. I remember older girls discussing Sister's lecture and saying it was filthy. "It's all about boys and Sister said to one girl that she would have twins."

Hearing the disgust in their voices I resolved never to go near that Sister and, when I was asked had Sister spoken to me, I said yes and hoped it wouldn't be checked. I was to step out into the world completely ignorant and, what I didn't know, open to sexual abuse.

40. OUT TO WORK, 1935

I was sent out on 7 November 1935 as a Companion Help, as were all the other girls. This was to imply that I was to be treated as one of the family and therefore my wages would be very low. Five shillings a week and my keep, and a further five shillings were paid into my Trust Account.

I was not to be left alone on the farm if my employers went away, I was to go with them or be sent back to Fairbridge. Fairbridge was trying to protect us from sexual abuse though I did not realise this.

Mostly our jobs were found close enough to the farm school for an after care officer to visit and check on our conditions. It would only be what the eye saw because no way would any complaints be listened to.[16] I was interviewed in front of my employer.

My going to church every Sunday was part of the agreement and my time was always to be supervised which meant I never had any time off and my life was controlled from rising in the morning till retiring at night. Whatever the working conditions my purpose was to stick to the job for twelve months, otherwise we were threatened with being sent to 'Gosnells'[17] which was a reform school for delinquent girls and I had heard horrible stories of that place.

Lake Grace, nearly two hundred miles south eastwards from Perth, was too far away for an after care officer to visit or for anybody to

---

[16] Complaints might be listened to but whether they were acted on was another matter. Geoffrey Thomas reported: "The travelling After-Care officer has very little power to help some of these unfortunate children."
[17] Geoffrey Thomas queried this disciplinary measure because 'the women and girls who go to Gosnells are as often as not street women and prostitutes. Can this be a fit and proper place for any Fairbridge girl?'

check the living conditions. I was given this job because it was considered unnecessary to visit me to check on my behaviour. It was all done by correspondence.

I was taken to Perth and put on a train for Lake Grace, my fare paid by my employer provided I stayed at the job for three months, otherwise it was repaid to them out of my wages. It was a night and day trip and the after care officer had found me a carriage with three other women travellers, so we were two to each side of the compartment, which enabled us to rest somewhat or rather sleep fitfully through the night.

One highlight of the trip was the lady who sat next to me, she had smiled and settled comfortably in the corner commenting that she liked travelling on trains as it was the only time she slept. I smiled and didn't really know how to answer her, let alone understand her.

Just before we were ready to settle down for the night she took this bottle out of her bag and asked both the other women to open it for her. They just shook their heads so she turned to me and asked: "Dear, could you take the lid off this bottle?" I smiled and took it from her and unscrewed the top, it was a flask of brandy. No wonder she always slept on trains.

I arrived at Lake Grace station by now completely confused about the time. I must have been very tired from the travelling and fear of the unknown.

Mr Robins was there with his utility truck to meet me and he sat me beside him as we drove back to his farm. He was ill with the flu and he told me he had to stop a few times to have a sip from his brandy bottle to enable him to keep going.

I remember seeing a rabbit run across the road and was excited. I could hear Miss Kittell's voice saying that if I saw a rabbit not to get excited so as not to let anyone know I was a country bumpkin! Even at that distance I could hear her admonishing me.

Lake Grace was a wheat growing area and the other Lakes near by were salt lakes, everybody talked of poverty, the farmers speaking of wheat being 10d a bushel (dry measure of eight gallons; nearly 37 litres). It was a foreign language to me, I just heard it without comprehending, I had been brought up on a farm school but trained to understand only housework.

Mrs Robins was a large lady and ex matron of a hospital where she had met her husband after a bad accident when he was tossed by his bull. He had a permanent hump on his back as a result and she, like all matrons of hospitals, was very overpowering. She did let me have some sleep on arrival for I must have looked as terrible as I felt. I believe I slept for two hours and was then awakened.

I thought I was waking up to breakfast, not dinner. I was sent outside to the rainwater tank to fetch drinking water. I saw the moon come up, the sky darken and the stars come out and I asked Mr Robins: "Does it always get dark in the morning?" I was looked at in puzzlement. As I peeled potatoes my mind was in chaos, until they both realised I had lost the day.

The house consisted of four rooms, the kitchen, a rouseabout's (farm labourer's) room, a lounge room up the passage and to its left the master bedroom. Mr and Mrs Robins had a baby son, Ben, and it was to look after him that I was really needed. He slept in his parents' room and I was to sleep in the lounge room, one narrow hard bed set against the wall.

It did not matter what time I wanted to go to bed, nobody left the lounge room or turned off the lights (kerosene lights). Nobody stopped their conversations and, even if other farmers came along to discuss wheat crop prices or other farming business, I was

137

given no consideration whatsoever. I was a chattel and as such was used, so much for the Companion Help and being treated as one of the family.

I had a drawer in the rouseabout's room where my clothes were kept, they didn't take much room. To bath, there was a large tin tub and this was placed in the rouseabout's room. The next part was to go to the dam and fill a bucket with water. This dam was created when a huge water hole was dug by a tractor and, like the rainwater tank, it also needed rain to keep it full.

The dam water was the colour of gravel and I took it to the kitchen and heated it in another bucket, a kerosene tin with wire handles, on the stove. As it heated I scooped off the scum as it rose to the top, like clarifying dripping. None of this really bothered me. It was heavy work and primitive yet at the same time a challenge.

What bothered me was having to bath in the rouseabout's room with no lock on the door and in no way being sure of my privacy. Once the rouseabout forgot and opened the door while I was in the bath. It was always a constant fear that this would happen and I could never enjoy having a bath.

I don't recall how Mr and Mrs Robins bathed, it must have been in their room. They were both bitter that their house was so poor, with no facilities, while the farm itself was full of so much expensive machinery. If tractors were not so expensive, they could add to the house. The price of wheat for them was a constant worry.

Mrs Robins was very hard on me, maybe because life was hard on her. I was always taking young Ben out in the pram to get him out of her way and give her peace. I loved young Ben but then I had a special way with children, I never found them trying.

One of my jobs was stringing the beans. I would take them outside and sit on the rainwater tank stand and prepare these for dinner with little Ben sitting in his pram. I sat on the wooden stand, as if on a bench, otherwise I had only the ground to sit on.

Mrs Robins showed me how to carefully cut very thinly down each side of the bean, no waste, until one day I found I could just string the beans, taking one end and pulling and the edge coming away, with even less waste. This caused a commotion and I was loudly harangued and had to do the beans all over again. The catch was if the beans were a bit old all the string didn't come off and you would get a mouthful as you ate. I didn't know that then.

The days were monotonously the same, I still got up at 5.30 am, lighted the fire, boiled kettles, cleaned the house, looked after Ben, prepared meals, washed up, did the washing in a copper outside.

The toilet was an outside pit system. It was similar to the pan system but there was no pan to empty. Newspaper would be set alight in the pit for cleansing. When the pit filled up, and it took a while, another would be built, the top part of the old one lifting free for the new one. I scrubbed the seat and kept it clean with plenty of disinfectant.

One evening when washing up I was drying a small silver sugar spoon and Mrs Robins was putting away because I could not reach the cupboard shelf, when she became aware the sugar spoon was missing. She asked me where the spoon was and the look on her face implied I had stolen it. I cheerily produced the spoon, joking: "Here is our spoon," and she snapped back at me about it being 'her spoon'.

I was being put back in my place as a servant in the household.

41. BREAKING THE FIRST RULE

Mr and Mrs Robins went into Lake Grace and left me on my own, so breaking the first rule of Fairbridge. I was given instructions on preparing the evening meal and was also asked to make an apple pie. I had never made one before, so I was told about the quantity of flour, dripping and wee bit of water etc and to put it in a hot oven.

I made the pie soon after their departure, rolled out the pastry, put it on the plate, filled it with apples, put its cover on top and brushed my hands clean, feeling very proud of myself as I put it in the oven.

Later I set the table and the vegetables were cooking when the Robinses came home. Mrs Robins inspected my work and asked for the apple pie, I told her it was in the oven and she had forgotten to tell me when to get it out. I didn't have a happy meal that night.

Another incident involved young Ben. For a week he spent his nights screaming in pain. I could not sleep and nor could anyone else but during the day I would still have to take him out, irrespective of the weather and quite often I myself was freezing, and try to find somewhere on the rainwater tank stand protected from the wind for myself and Ben while Mrs Robins slept. I would continue with my duties and try to comfort Ben.

Finally Mrs Robins took Ben to the Doctor. He was diagnosed as having a mastoid in both ears and had been going through unnecessary pain.

I was shown how to grist wheat for porridge, coarse or fine, though I mostly liked it coarse with that lovely chewing feeling as you bit on the porridge. It was such a delicious flavour when served with warm milk fresh that morning from the cow. I never minded standing outside gristing the wheat.

One of the cooking jobs I was taught was always a nightmare. It was mock fish and was a very easy dish consisting of a beaten egg or two, according to quantity required, and grated potatoes dropped into the egg mixture with pepper and salt added.

Grated potatoes quickly dissolve into water and so, with hot dripping already in the pan, the mixture had to be quickly placed in tablespoon heaps in the fat and, when brown, turned over until cooked. They were then put in the oven until all was ready and served with tomato sauce.

This dish was agony for me because if one flake of that potato broke away in the cooking there would be a huge commotion and I was stood over as I tried to gather the offending flake and make it rejoin the cake. At the same time, I would be told that my mixture was turning to liquid and that I was not quick enough to get the cakes cooked.

Despite all this, I enjoyed them served with bread and butter at the evening meal. My tablespoon measure had to be exact too, no bigger or smaller than the one to come or the one before.

The laundry was always done outside in an open copper and because of my size, I was well supervised to prevent an accident.

There was a Fairbridge boy, John Acol, who had been sent to work on the farming side of things. He was good to me and was there to be taught about the sheep and wheat, the Fairbridge training being so basic.

I saw very little of John as his conditions were worse than mine but his treatment was no different from that of rouseabouts of that time. His quarters were at the end of a tin shed, no conveniences at all. His bed was a horsehair mattress on a wire frame with grey Army blankets, no sheets of any kind and a pillow devoid of pillowslip.

The washing facilities were water in an enamel dish. The water in the mornings was cold and I know myself that ice sometimes set on the top of the water for washing. I just broke the ice before splashing my face and rubbing dry. John would have done the same. He boiled his own billy and fetched his meals from the house. It was not considered right to think of a rouseabout as a person, they were there to work hard and grow up tough.

Now John often had to walk across paddocks checking on lambs that may have been abandoned by their mothers and I would often go with him. There was a time when I was bottle feeding seven lambs. I was very scared of the rams especially when they started to fight each other, rushing and banging their heads with such impact they could be heard for miles. When this happened, John would walk me round the long way till we got to the lambing sheep.

During these walks, John taught me songs and we had a wonderful time singing together the Teddy Bears' Picnic, I knew it all after a few walks. It was here I learnt to ride a bike and it was while I was learning to ride that some of the pet lambs rushed towards me as I was going down a slight hill and I ended up in the barbed wire fence, tearing my frock and scratching myself through to my stomach.

Another day when I was intending to take a short cut through the same fence in a storm, suddenly a flash of lightning ran right along the top of the fence. I gave up the idea and learnt another valuable lesson, to keep away from metal in a storm.

I enjoyed those walks with John and not knowing about the mating of humans or animals, I would avoid looking at them when John told me that the rams had been put in with the sheep for this purpose. I thought it was all wrong to see, I was embarrassed, and it would not have entered my head to ask questions.

It was here also that I heard of the death of my friend, Marjorie Rick, whom we called 'Rickie', we used to correspond when working. The letters from Fairbridge told me nothing but one of the girls, who lived close by and had worked with her, told me that Rickie had been found lying on the kitchen floor where she worked, rolling around in agony and that she died in agony of tuberculosis of the bowel.

I could never check on this. I knew of tuberculosis of the lungs and it is only now that I wonder was it a growth in the bowel. It took me a long time to forget Rickie's death. She had always been a happy person and I could well imagine that she never mentioned her pain for fear of being disbelieved or, when she mentioned it, having it dismissed. I can weep for her now even as I write, yet then I was fatalistic about it all.

We had all been long accustomed to this type of treatment and there was no way of getting away from the system. Until we were twenty one[18] we were all tied to Fairbridge, it was all we had.

---

[18] This is what most of the children believed and after-care staff were also led to understand that this was legal as well as moral control. Not so, according to a solicitor consulted by Tempe Woods. Legally, the children were out of Fairbridge control at 18 although for their own protection they and anyone else could be 'bluffed' otherwise.

42. OLD FAIRBRIDGIANS TOGETHER

I returned to Fairbridge for my annual holidays to stay at the Old Fairbridgians' Club House, which had been specially built for this purpose. It contained two wings of cubicles, one for the boys and one for the girls. The centre of the building consisted of three rooms all with sliding walls.

One side of the communal dining room was the boys' common room and other side the girls' common room, we were never supposed to sit together even on holidays. We were all growing up, however, and the boys' common room was rarely used as they would come and join us.

The Club House was in the charge of a manager and manageress who still treated us like children, children who could do wrong and bad things such as get sexually attracted to each other. This was something that had not entered my thinking and neither had I physically felt any need so I had no curiosity about it. I would jump nervously if one of the boys even put his arm around my waist and laughingly step aside.

The boys told me much later I had been nicknamed 'Touchy'. Some of the boys said that though they would have liked to approach me I had a look that stopped them, they said: "Not you, Florrie, we wouldn't have tried anything with you."

The annual holidays were compulsory, as were the holidays at Fairbridge. On one of my visits two Old Fairbridgians who were engaged to be married told the manager they were going for a walk and he forbade it. I can still hear them pleading with him but he was adamant. Finally, Lilly became exasperated and burst out:

144

"I know what you're finking, you're finking filthy fings." She was too wound up to speak correctly, but what I did enjoy was to see them take off on their walk and damn the consequences.

If the manager forbade us to meet together in the girls' common room, we would all go outside and sit on the stoep. Fairbridge was originally going to be in Rhodesia (now Zimbabwe) and Kingsley Fairbridge was originally from South Africa, hence the South African terms and expressions.[19] The malaria mosquito, we were told, put a stop to the idea.[20]

I visited my Cottage Mother to tell her all about my job even though we had corresponded regularly. What I was unaware of was that she was pumping me about my work and living conditions, my sleeping and bathing arrangements in particular.

What I also didn't know was that Miss Kittell did not like how I was living and went along and saw the new Principal (A. D. Paterson), and asked that I not be sent back to Lake Grace.

With the exception of leaving John, because all the boys were like brothers to us and very kind, I was not sorry not to return. Apparently I looked very pale and not at all well and there was enough change in me to give concern.

---

[19] Ruby Fairbridge said (Fairbridge Farm, p. 43) that the Chartered Company of Rhodesia refused a grant of land because it considered Rhodesia too young a country for the inception of a farm school.
[20] It was in Rhodesia, Kingsley Fairbridge said (Autobiography; London, 1927, p. 14), that he suffered the first of lifelong attacks of malaria. He was aged about 11.

Correspondence was already being exchanged regarding a new job and I was asked only one question, whether I would like to work in the city or the country. I chose the country because I knew there was a job close to one of my farm school friends who had asked me to try and get it.

The policy was to keep us away from friends in case we became 'slapdash' at our jobs, no thought that happiness could make us better workers. It was also policy that no child under sixteen years be sent to employment in the city. It was felt they weren't mature enough to handle 'city life' and city employers were not so ready to play nursemaid to us during our 'time off' or supervise where we should go.

These were all the requirements of employing a Fairbridge girl and I was fifteen years of age but still that title stuck, 'a credit to the school and trustworthy'. No one understood about my feeling of insecurity (which I still have), I looked and was capable but it was a false cloak I wore.

So I was sent to the city. On 27 October 1936, I started working for Mr and Mrs Plaistowe at Peppermint Grove, a wealthy suburb of Perth. In the meantime, correspondence is going on between Lake Grace and Fairbridge about me not going back and why.

My job at Peppermint Grove was to last two years. Mr Plaistowe picked me up from the station and drove me to my job. He was very fair to me while Mrs Plaistowe (as with most women employers) was not. She was too demanding of my time. I was expected to be good at everything I did, there was no room for

146

learning or for mistakes. I really was always on edge. Strangely enough, I have no recollection of the little girl I was supposed to handle so well. It is the housework that looms large in my memory. After the last job I found this one more enjoyable.

To begin with, I had a nice little room in a kind of attic. I liked its shape and the window just behind my bed I remember well. I was happy in my own room shut off from the world and communication with other people. I tried to write some poetry which ended up going nowhere, mostly my days were too long working and I was too tired to do anything but sleep at night. Sleep was my escape from the hurts of the world and I was always able to sleep well.

I would arise about 6 am and prepare breakfast for the family. Mr Plaistowe would go off to work, they owned a chocolate import business in the city. Mrs Plaistowe had her round of social engagements and my job was to look after their home and daughter.

It was at Plaistowes' that I began to appreciate fine things like furniture, table linen, china and glassware and good cutlery. It never later in life made me envious of these things but I was always able to appreciate and enjoy the beauty of such living and, given the opportunity, would have loved to do things with the best I could have. I enjoyed setting the table, with a blanket under the tablecloth known as a silencer and everything gleaming ready for a dinner engagement.

My joy was inside myself, I could not share this in words, I was acutely conscious of my menial role. I could not see how I could rise above my position as the maid. I craved to satisfy my need for literature in all its forms and longed for an opportunity to 'better myself'.

At Plaistowes' I started to learn to cook, Lake Grace wasn't what I call cooking, Plaistowes' was gourmet, good quality food etc. It

147

must have come easily to me for I have no memories of distress. My day ended when I was no longer needed so whenever there was a dinner party, and this occurred quite regularly, if there were ten or more to dinner it would be almost midnight before I retired.

The dining room was immediately off the kitchen and any sounds of activity in the kitchen were not allowed to be heard in the dining room. If this occurred, Mrs Plaistowe would come out and very crossly tell me off. This meant I was not supposed to wash up until dinner was over. Mrs Plaistowe would then come out and I would take coffee into the lounge room and was then free to wash up.

This was agony. I could scarcely keep awake as it was just standing in the kitchen while each course was consumed and waiting to clear away and take in the next. I developed a way of working without a sound, I would run the water into the sink oh so quietly, easily done after a little practice, and then wash every dish singly, no stacking where the clink of china on china could be heard.

I remember vividly the night Mrs Plaistowe came out to tell me I could wash up now and then she saw the kitchen completely tidy and everything put away. There was a look of disbelief on her face and she asked me who I had in the kitchen helping me. I told her nobody and felt I wasn't believed but from that time onwards, I would quietly wash up while dinner was on and at least I got to bed at 11 o'clock instead of midnight.

This sort of scheming naturally took its toll on the nervous system. I was always afraid of being caught out and recall one night after such an event going upstairs to bed but in the early hours of the morning feeling very ill.

I got out of bed to walk downstairs to the toilet but was swaying all over the stairs and trying hard not to make a sound. I must have been moaning in distress, for Mrs Plaistowe called out in her usual cross voice: "Florence, what's wrong?" I managed to reply that I was ill, but she never came to see if I needed help as I reached the bottom of the stairs and stumbled into the bathroom. I all but fainted and was violently ill. I was there for nearly an hour before I had the balance and the energy to walk back upstairs.

The next day I was on duty again, feeling weak and washed out and all the sympathy I received was to be asked what was wrong with me last night. The rules of Fairbridge were that if you needed medical or dental attention, your employer saw to this, bills then being sent to Fairbridge. I was never sent for a check up to see if anything was wrong.

I can remember sitting on the stairs talking to Mr Plaistowe about my ambition to write, I wanted to do that as well as be a Kindergarten teacher.

He was the only person who ever asked me what I was reading and tried to give me some clues on how to do what I wanted to do. But I wasn't given the time or place, I was too tired to think let alone write. Everybody knew what I wanted to do, the after care officer, my Cottage Mother, but nobody placed my feet on the right path. I might have gone into journalism, I think.

To add to my work Mrs Plaistowe had to have an operation for appendicitis and I had the house to run and her daughter to look after. I didn't mind at all, there was a sort of peace. I was able to work at my own pace and still get everything done.

Then Mr Plaistowe's mother was unable to look after her own flat, after she had a fall, and he asked me nicely if I would mind going and cleaning the place on a regular basis and that I would be paid extra. I liked his mother and didn't mind but now I was really busy.

One thing I loved was going with my employers to their asparagus farm, up in the hills, where Mr Plaistowe checked on the production and his workers. Lots of people were employed there and when we arrived at the cottage, bunches of fresh asparagus would be waiting for us.

By this time I knew how to cook it and serve it with a sauce of melted butter. How delicious it was. I, of course, always ate in the kitchen. We regularly went to the cottage.

Miss Fryer-Smith (left), Domestic Science Teacher, and Mrs Clarke, school teacher, walking in the hills at Fairbridge

44. INNOCENCE LED ME INTO TROUBLE

I learnt to work quietly around the house, Mrs Plaistowe's friends were not to be disturbed by the domestic, which meant I could appear unexpectedly and not always at the right moment.

There was a Doctor friend of Mrs Plaistowe who used to come around regularly. I thought nothing of it, he was a family friend and that was that. To begin with I was too unworldly to suspect something was wrong, therefore my innocence led me into trouble.

This particular day I went into the dining room to dust. Without a sound I opened the door and was actually at the table dusting before Mrs Plaistowe with her Doctor friend saw me, and quite naturally so as he was busy kissing her. I carried on with what I was doing, however understandably Mrs Plaistowe and the Doctor were disturbed.

I thought nothing of it as love and sex were not part of my life. In fact if Mrs Plaistowe hadn't tried to explain what had been going on, I would never have had a suspicion. After the Doctor had gone, she came to me to explain that she had given him a kiss of comfort as he was dying of radiation sickness caused by his work. I tried to tell her not to worry, I didn't know what all the concern was about.

Our relationship was never the same, I think she was always worried that I may say something to Mr Plaistowe. She made me promise I would never speak about it to anyone.

I was supposed to have regular time off but, apart from going with Mr and Mrs Plaistowe wherever they went, I did not have any special time to myself. My life was completely given to them. From

151

the time I left Fairbridge, my sport and my singing had all come to an abrupt end. As a consequence of all these things and the fact I was always on edge, my health began to suffer.

One Sunday morning I woke up and stepped out of bed to perform my usual chores when this excruciating pain in my groin doubled me up. There were red blisters in my groin, too sore to touch and too sore to let me walk. I simply couldn't get out of bed. Finally, Mrs Plaistowe came up the stairs and crossly asked me why I wasn't up.

I explained that I was in pain and showed her my groin and the blisters. She asked me to get up and I tried to stand and couldn't. She told me to stay in bed and added that I was upsetting the routine by not looking after her daughter, or making her early cup of tea and family breakfast.

She went downstairs and I lay there in pain waiting for it to go away, hoping I could then carry on and please her. It was quite some time later that she brought me a cup of tea and a slice of bread, setting it down angrily beside me, telling me: "I am not here to look after you."

She asked to see my legs again and I did so, embarrassed, for I also had my period. She told me she couldn't ask the Doctor to come and see me that day as it was Sunday, he would be playing golf and she couldn't ask him to give up his game.

I was lying there in great pain being treated like a naughty child refusing to get up. No painkillers of any sort and at the mercy of Mrs Plaistowe's care. I was left and not a considerate word was uttered. I lay there quietly crying to myself and it must have been 2 o'clock in the afternoon when the family Doctor (this was not Mrs Plaistowe's Doctor friend) finally arrived.

I often wonder whether it was Mr Plaistowe who insisted on me having medical treatment. The Doctor came upstairs with Mrs Plaistowe and diagnosed shingles and then asked Mrs Plaistowe to leave the room so he could talk to me.

He was very kindly towards me and asked: "What days do you have off work?" I replied honestly that I didn't have any days off and went everywhere with Mr and Mrs Plaistowe. He then asked: "What girlfriends do you have of your own age that you visit?" and whether I went to the pictures or dancing or out with friends.

I told him I did none of these things but that I did take Sox the dog for a walk in the afternoon. (Mrs Plaistowe used to often send me to walk the dog saying it was 'blowing the cobwebs away'.) I told him I also went to the beach with the Plaistowes and their child to swim with them.

Little did I know that the Doctor was concerned about my work arrangements. He told me to stay in bed for a few days and then went downstairs. What he said I can only piece together by Mrs Plaistowe's reaction, for after the Doctor had gone she came upstairs, quite furious, and attacked me verbally.

She told me the Doctor had said I needed to stay in bed for a few days and that she wasn't going to look after me so I would have to go back to Fairbridge. She also told me the Doctor had insisted that I go out more with people my own age, and that I should have at least half a day off a week and more free time.

On, and on, and on she went, while I lay there helpless. The Doctor had told her I was under great stress and was to be encouraged to play and relax more. All I remember of that day was the Doctor's kindness and Mrs Plaistowe's anger.

I went away for a while to recuperate and thanks to my Fairbridge file (eventually sent to me), I apparently stayed with Miss Kittell somewhere, as well as at Fairbridge. She was always very concerned if I became ill.

I remember this break only because Mrs Plaistowe employed a non Fairbridge woman to relieve in my position and she was given my room to use. Now my sister in England every year used to send me a necklace for my birthday and I had a lovely collection of these hanging on the dressing table. When I came back, they were all missing. I told Mrs Plaistowe because I was very upset over this and I valued them, but she told me no one would take them and I must have lost them.

Fairbridge asked me to visit a Fairbridge girl living in a small flat close by. I used to walk and see her, she was very poor and struggling with a baby. I often put money in her gas meter so she could cook or get some heat, but it was the type of poverty I would have hated. She looked forward to my visits, they broke the monotony of her life.

I remember one visit, someone had given me a crepe de chine frock in a pale blue which fitted me well and I rather liked it. On the way home it started to rain and crepe de chine cannot take water without shrinking. There I was running home as fast as I could with this dress shrinking up and in. I tugged at it as it tightened across my breasts and finally tugged so hard it split down the front.

Fortunately, I wasn't far from home and ran inside and up to my room. That was the end of the dress for though I ironed it back to

154

size, I could not mend invisibly the tear down the front and I never wore crepe de chine again.

After my attack of shingles I went each morning with Mr Plaistowe, Ted as I was soon to think of him although I always addressed him as 'Mr', to swim at Cottesloe beach. He used to swim each morning before work and as part of my relaxation therapy it was suggested he take me along, not that I have ever been good in the surf and I prefer to be able to swim in still water.

It was good and exhilarating although his wife was never really happy about this freedom for me. It was while we went swimming that I was able to have many intelligent conversations with him. I did discuss literature among other things, but we also discussed the state of the world and whether there would be a second world war.

I remember Ted Plaistowe confirming there would be a war and this frightened me and how I hoped he would be wrong. He made me feel like a person of substance and not a domestic worker of little intelligence.

I started to ask Fairbridge for a move before I told Mrs Plaistowe I wanted to move on. She was becoming harder and harder to work for.

At that time my knowledge of banking – and my awe of banks and those who worked in those austere places – was shockingly limited, and because of this ignorance and feeling of inferiority, I could not bring myself to ask questions about banking and how it worked.

Consequently, I thought that if I was going to leave Perth and go to the country to work, I would have to draw all my money and rebank it wherever I was. I knew nothing about transfers, therefore when I knew I had only a couple more weeks left with the Plaistowes I went to the bank and timidly took out all my money, not much, probably only about £20 or £30, but I felt so small and insignificant and I can still see the look of disbelief on the face of the teller as I withdrew all my money.

The sequel to this act of mine was played out in the Plaistowes' kitchen. I was busily cooking when she came in from wherever she had been and asked me why I had drawn all my money out of the bank. Now I was really angry. Who in the bank knew me and knew her and had reported my private business to her? She had no right to know. I told her that I was leaving in two weeks' time and that's why I had drawn out the money.

It ended up with her telling me that I had only used her home as a boarding house and that I could pack up and leave tomorrow, and that she would ring Fairbridge and tell them what train I would be on. I left hurt but pleased. I really had had all I could take.

Fairbridge would never know the full story, I would never tell the reason for my early departure because of the threat of being sent to Gosnells if we were sacked or did not stay at a job for twelve months.

Fortunately, Mr Plaistowe had written favourably about my work for the two years I had been in their employ. I acted as I knew Fairbridge would have expected me to act, never really telling the truth because nobody wanted to hear it.

Back at Fairbridge enjoying a long earned rest, I looked forward to working again in the country. I spent my time socialising with other Old Fairbridgians on holiday, walking down to the river and strolling beside it, sometimes alone, sometimes with some of the girls and sometimes with the boys, strolling back to my old picnic ground in the hills.

I visited Miss Kittell in her cottage, being treated as an adult and not as a kid. But this didn't rest easy with me because I was conscious of having been one of her charges, suffering what they now were suffering. I used to try and call in every day for a while but teenagers are selfish individuals and this particular day (in August 1938) I decided I wanted to do something else, take a walk in the bush or whatever.

I never called in to see her and she died that day. The senior girls told me that she came home from lunch in the Staff Dining Room, sat in her chair beside the bed, put her feet on the bed and quietly died.

She deserved such a peaceful end for the little she did tell me implied that she had had a very hard life in Germany, being expelled and living in Poland till something brought her to Australia as a Governess. She called herself 'a Polish German' and her favourite taunt was to call me a 'German flathead', the greatest insult she could throw at me.

I never realised her concern for me, not then, not until 1989-90 when my counsellor led me to look at the part she had played in my life.

Even when she was trying to train me to step out of an orphanage and to enter society as a 'lady', able to mix with anybody, her ultimate aim being for me to make a good marriage after a good education, all I was aware of was her strict discipline, her harshness, her exasperation at mistakes.

It was my loyalty to her as my Cottage Mother, not any love of her, that kept me returning to her and because I had not learnt to say no to any request as this was always sternly punished. Consequently I accepted all requests from her.

If she had lived until I was older, perhaps her influence would have guided me further. I was seventeen years old when she died, immature, mixed up, just out to please Fairbridge and every job I was sent to. I knew no other life, while feeling even then despair with the lack of intelligent development in a life completely dominated by other people's needs.

I had nightmares the night she died. I saw her all night gliding through these trees, high above my head, and I didn't know what she wanted of me. She left me £100 in her will. Looking back now, it is strange that I was back at Fairbridge on holiday when her time to leave this world arrived. I believe she was seventy five or six.

Since my return to Fairbridge in 1987, I discovered that to a lot of my cottage girls, she was a figure of fear. To me she was a dominating force, she was cruel, yes, unfair, yes, and this does not go down well with children. She was also full of culture and tried to give us, in her own way, a taste for good music and literature, but what hope had she of improving our lot.

Rest in peace Katharine Kittell . . . and would that I could talk to you now from my new found depth of understanding, for the cruel system you and I were involved in was not of your making.

47. DAMBORING

I cannot remember how I travelled to Damboring except by reading my file which indicates it was by night train. It was over one hundred miles north eastwards from Perth. I can even now picture that brick home with its large underground water tank. This was a farmer who was not extremely poor like so many farmers were.

It was good to be back in the country and good to be free of the responsibility of other people's children because one was limited in how far one could go to discipline a child who was rude and spiteful. This household was Mr and Mrs Sutcliffe, myself and their worker Mr Robinson, known as Robbie but to me always Mr Robinson.

Once the land was in your blood as it was with me, it was the only place worth being. To me the city with its twinkling lights, food places of cakes and meats, was a reason to dress prettily to walk down the paved streets and see a life different to the country, but it took only a day to satisfy my need for change.

I used to enjoy taking in my fill of the fairy lights as we drove away in the evening to return to the farm, there to unpack the month's supply of groceries before the next needed visit. The town we used to travel to was Dalwallinu, it was these names, Damboring and Dalwallinu that I loved so well and never forgot, for the locals used to say Damboring was just that, damn boring.

I had my own room, not the light interesting room as at the Plaistowes', this was off the back verandah, almost the size of a very small hall. It contained a single hard mattress bed against the right hand wall as I opened the door, about the door's length away, on the floor a very small round mat to step on when getting out of bed and, almost in reach of the bed, a black stained combined dressing table and wardrobe.

This black furniture was to depress me and put me 'in the dumps' as we would say at Fairbridge, and to add to the feeling of extreme poverty that the room bore to me was a light with only a forty watt globe, probably because they generated their own electricity. There was one small window in the room.

The effect of this was to sink so deeply into my subconscious that in later years, when I was out of the care of Fairbridge, if I was taken to or had to stay in a hotel, such a depression would fall on me. I would get into such a state of mind that in no way could I go into that room except to sleep.

One time, trying to get me to overcome this reaction, I was taken by a concerned friend to the then best hotel in Adelaide. I walked through the front doors, the reception area done out in rich colours, luxurious chairs and tasteful decor, yet as soon as I entered my room and the door was shut, never mind who was with me to look after me, within half an hour I would be lying on the bed weeping my heart out.

Even to this day, I like a feeling of outdoor living, I must feel I can get outside, I must feel free and not closed in, closed in becomes dark and alone. Though I was classified as Companion Help and some of my time off was supposedly shared with the family, reading or sewing or listening to the wireless, my home was that room, that bedroom, that was where I belonged and that was all I had in the world. The feeling there was oh so different to how I felt in my room at Plaistowes'.

My day started as always, boiling the kettle for Mrs Sutcliffe's early morning cup of tea. Mr Sutcliffe would come and knock on my door each morning and call out: "Florence, are you awake?" I would roll over, climb out of bed and dress. Mr Sutcliffe would then sit on the verandah, put on his shoes and attend to his jobs. He had already lighted the fire for me in the wood stove and the kettle was beginning to boil.

Mrs Sutcliffe was supposed not to be too well. I didn't know why and her lying in bed in the mornings and the cup of tea were part of her invalid treatment.

This house contained a bathroom, with a plumbed in bath, a real luxury on farms then. I was told I could have a bath once a week, just a few inches of water in the bath provided the tank contained enough water, otherwise it was a quick rinse in the bathroom handbasin. This conserving of water never worried me, only it seemed a pity to have such a great bath and not be able to use it.

Breakfast was always a big mainly fried meal for working men, chops, eggs, sausages, porridge, toast, some or all of these foods. Chops were always cooked until crisp and crunchy, gravy always poured over the top. Left over vegetables were turned into bubble and squeak, all mashed and fried together. Porridge was hard gristed wheat which I liked above all things. Eggs and milk were from the farm itself.

I had two men to cook for, Mr Sutcliffe and old Robbie. Robbie when I first arrived resented me greatly, he had no time for women or even me as a young girl and at first he gave me a very rough time. He usually came in early for his breakfast as was befitting the farm hand and ate on his own. He ate well and heartily criticised me the whole time, my clothes, my hair or whatever else he could find.

Now Robbie's life was his horses, he drove a team of four draught horses nearly every day and I thought him very brave, especially recalling my experience with the bolting draught horses at Fairbridge. He groomed those horses so that you thought they were going to parade down London streets. He was kind and loving to horses and woe betide anybody who spoke roughly to them or about them or, if it came to that, even touched them.

Robbie was a big stubborn man but nearly eighty years old and the Sutcliffes used to wonder what would happen one day if those horses took it into their heads to bolt, there would be no holding them and he would be killed, but this never happened.

Nobody in the world came up to his love and admiration of his horses, till one day Robbie came into the kitchen to have his breakfast and I did the usual, feeding him well, accepting his remarks and answering back to him when he said: "Florrie, you're as pretty as a picture, just like my horses."

No greater praise could any woman get than to be likened to his horses, however incongruous I felt it was.

The hissing of the new petrol irons scared the life out of Flo.   Sketch and description by Mavis Hayes

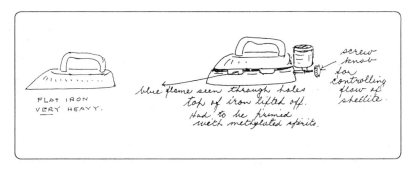

FLAT IRON
VERY HEAVY.

blue flame seen through holes
top of iron lifted off.
Had to be primed
with methylated spirits.

screw
knob
for
controlling
flow of
shellite.

48. MAKING SOAP FROM DRIPPING

Though Mrs Sutcliffe was suffering from ill health, she was never an invalid once she was up for breakfast and managed to find all manner of jobs for me to do and keep busy all day. I was allowed an hour's break after lunch and would go thankfully to my room, lie down exhausted and fall asleep, but oh not for long.

It had to be deliberate on Mrs Sutcliffe's part, though I never wanted to believe it, for not more than half an hour's rest would have been taken when she would start gardening in the hard soil, using a hoe and hitting the ground with large thumps and always just outside my room.

I would try to ignore it and her but why did my conscience always make me feel I was meant to be out there with her, giving a hand? I would drag myself off the bed and struggle outside and ask if I could help. She would never tell me to go back and rest, instead I was handed the hoe and together we would work in the garden.

I learnt to make soap, clarifying the dripping once it was past using for cooking. This took a long time, boiling it up day after day till the dripping was cleaned of all impurities. It was then placed in the outside copper, brought to the desired temperature and caustic soda carefully added, causing it to froth up and bubble over almost immediately. One false move and a horrible burn could be received to the skin and eyes, the eyes were really the danger. When cool enough, the mixture was poured into trays using a very large ladle or dipper before being cut into blocks.

All the washing was done in the outside copper, it was heavy work lifting it out with the copper stick, putting it in the trough, rinsing, then dipping into the blue water rinse. We had a bag of blue powder, about an inch round and an inch deep, dipped into the second rinse to make the clothes look whiter. Finally the washing was put through the mangle to squeeze out as much water as possible and then I would hang it on the line.

Starching was a horrible job, making that starch so no lumps would form, but worse still was ironing those starched clothes, how the iron suffered if too much starch was added to the collars of the shirts. It took an age to iron starched tablecloths and all with flat irons heated on the stove or the new petrol irons, whose noise as they hissed away would frighten the life out of me. Washdays were truly heavy days.

I learnt butter making too, firstly putting the milk into the urn and separating the milk from the cream and keeping the cream until there was enough to make a wad of butter. I preserved the cream in a big urn by adding saltpetre.

I would beat the cream by hand. I found it much easier, placing the cream in a large bowl, making sure I had an apron to protect my dress even if it was only a work dress, because it became very greasy. I would patiently beat the cream, waiting for what seemed never to want to happen, the final separation of the butter from the butter fat. I would then wash the butter till it ran clean of butter milk and finally add salt and shape the butter.

Sometimes the cream had started to turn and the rancid flavour would go through the butter which would then be used for cooking, as it could be disguised by other flavours such as vanilla or cocoa.

One flavour we could never disguise was that of preserved eggs. Eggs were collected when very fresh and a substance like Vaseline called Keepit or waterglass was rubbed over the eggs to close the pores and keep out the bacteria. We could lay down eggs this way for over twelve months but sometimes if the chooks (hens) hadn't been laying well that season, the preserved eggs would be stored longer than usual and though they weren't bad, they developed a strong peculiar flavour.

I didn't like them but the people on the land appeared not to notice. We used them in scrambled eggs because it was almost impossible to separate the white from the yolk.

We also used them in making sponge cakes though it took a lot more beating of the eggs to get the thick creamy substance. The large sumptuous sponge was then filled with jam and home whipped cream and taken reverently to the tennis days, country people's relaxing days, each person trying to have the tallest sponge cake there.

I became very clever under supervision in this culinary delight and even if the sponge was slightly tainted with the flavour of preserved eggs, nobody referred to it.

I had been told, when taking this job, about the tennis club not far away but was not allowed to attend on my own. When our employers wanted to, they carried out Fairbridge's instructions to the letter. We were not to be left alone or go without supervision. I went to the tennis but only with the Sutcliffes. I had no racquet of my own and had to hope somebody might lend me one.

Sufficient to say I rarely played but I was very useful looking after everyone's children and helping set up afternoon tea.

I remember travelling in the back of the utility to the tennis days and all the rabbits everywhere, so thick they were and so still sitting on the bare earth that I used to say a person could scoop them up as the utility went past. There were burrows as far as the eye could see, the rabbits had well and truly beaten the farmer.

49. A NASTY RUMOUR

Fairbridge's instructions could be forgotten when it did not suit, such as the time the Sutcliffes had to go away for a few days and naturally I was left to look after Robbie as far as his food went.

Strictly speaking, I should not have been left alone, especially where men or boys were around and there were other men working on the place. I was frightened because I slept in that house all on my own with my room easily accessible from the verandah.

Nothing happened but there was a nasty rumour. Mr and Mrs Sutcliffe returned four days after leaving and I went out to meet them to see if I could do anything, bring in groceries as they had brought quite a lot back from Perth. This could be a year's supply of bulk food.

I became aware of their strange attitude towards me, followed by stranger questions such as what had I done while they were away, where had I been, had I stayed on the farm all the time? I innocently answered these questions because I had been nowhere and had done nothing but work. Finally it all came out, somebody had told them that I had gone out one night with a boy but because I had not done what he wanted, I had been left to walk four miles home and hadn't got back till the early hours of the morning.

Though I denied it vehemently and for the life of me could not imagine how such a story started, I always felt I was never believed and they really watched me for a while as if expecting any day I was going to become pregnant. I often wondered later if Robbie had started the story in the hope of getting rid of me.

166

I shall never know why it was circulated, I was so ignorant and unaware of my developing womanhood. That other people were observing this and speculating about me distressed me.

I remember those large ploughed paddocks that surrounded the house, every vestige of foliage removed, no hedges, mallee roots stacked in great heaps, burnt where they were or carted in for use in the house. I walked across these paddocks with food for the men, tea in the billy and something solid to eat. I loved it and whenever I was allowed to do this chore I would sing aloud as I walked, feeling a sense of freedom.

I will always remember the fear I felt when the wind whipped up the soil from those paddocks, as from inside the house you could see a dark black cloud reaching from the earth to the heavens till everything was as black as night. Mrs Sutcliffe and I would race to shut every window and door as the wind blew this monster towards us. We put draught excluders at the crack of each door but nothing stopped that black giant from hurling itself with full force at the house and there was nothing we could do but wait for the fury to die.

When it did, the black dust was indescribable. It was called a dust storm but it was Australia's topsoil disappearing forever. They say it blew all the way to New Zealand.

We were left to shovel it out of the house, the inches of soil had settled over everything. It was so incredible, I wrote a poem about it and sent it to the Old Fairbridgians' magazine. I watched this tragedy happen more than once or twice, mainly during a dry summer although at any season if the weather was dry. The grit would be in our hair, our clothes, our mouth and it took days of curtain washing, of dusting and polishing before things returned to normal.

One time when the men were busy in the paddocks, Mrs Sutcliffe decided that around the house needed tidying as some grass had grown long and it was dry enough to burn. I've always had a healthy respect for fires, especially in the dry Australian atmosphere.

I was wishing she wouldn't do it till the men came home but do it she did and for a while all was well till a gust of wind started. Suddenly our small fire was racing towards the open gates and a paddock full of ripe wheat.

We had bags and were beating with all our might at this fire but it was getting away from us. I was really scared and Mrs Sutcliffe began to panic. The men had seen what was happening and were with us in a flash. The fire was only stopped seconds away from a disaster. I felt as if I was guilty as Mr Sutcliffe started to voice his opinion on such a stupid action.

It was here that I learnt the art of chutney and jam making and all kinds of preserves. Boxes of apples, bags of onions, ripe tomatoes, all bought cheaply in season or acquired from some other farmer. I used to love mincing those apples and onions though one did have weepy eyes over the onions. It was the time of inexpensive dried sultanas, currants and raisins and these would be added to the apple chutney.

The smell was delicious. Plum chutney and pickles were great to serve with cold meats and a salad. Cold meats were always plentiful because of the cooking of legs and shoulders of farm killed sheep. Everything was tasty and fresh and good to eat.

I also learnt how to make and bake bread starting from making our own yeast from potato water and hops. I loved the smell of those hops. We put a large potato in a pint of water with a teaspoon of hops and boiled it for twenty minutes. It was strained, cooled slightly, then a tablespoon of flour and of sugar added. Yeast was poured into old beer bottles, it should work in a few hours in a bottle previously used for yeast or twenty four hours in a new bottle.

A fig or raisin added to the yeast would make it work more quickly. New corks were tightly sealed, yet during the night you would hear the loud explosions as the cork was expelled from the bottle. Finally using the yeast to make the bread, that great farmhouse smell, crusty loaves eaten warm on baking day and then stored for the best part of the week till baking day came around again.

These were joyous real life moments for me. It was after one such baking day that I nicked my leg against a roughly opened tin and Mrs Sutcliffe told me to put some Carbolic on it, an antiseptic solution. I went into the large pantry and saw a bottle labelled 'Carbolic Acid'. I didn't know there were two different Carbolics on the shelf, one the antiseptic, the other the acid.

I generously dabbed my leg with the acid and in a little while was jumping around in pain as the scratch and surrounds were now all blisters. Something further was dabbed on my leg after discussion with Mrs Sutcliffe, who gave me a long lecture about my stupidity. Apart from my leg smarting for a very long time, I suffered no ill effects and learnt about Carbolic acid.

The Sutcliffes had a galvanised iron roof, which most homes did in those days, with the roof becoming flatter as it ran into the guttering to collect the rain that did fall and keep the underground tank as full as possible. All around was a verandah of criss cross slats and Mrs Sutcliffe decided both the roof and this lattice work of the verandah needed painting. I, of course, was to do the painting, the men being much too busy with their farm work to find time for such tasks.

Ladder and paint were provided and up I climbed with paint and brush to do as I was asked. It must have been late spring or early summer for I was not on that roof very long when it became too hot for me to sit on. I clambered down the ladder announcing it was too hot but was provided with a wheat bag to sit on and sent back up. I didn't really mind it, though it was a bit scary, but the heat was uncomfortable making it almost impossible to paint. Each day I went up there till it was finished.

Then I had to paint the lattice work and what a job. Before long I was seeing double as the pattern became a blur and I had to do it properly, none of your slapping on the paint and hoping for the best. It was not meant to run and had to look good when finished. I worked hard and consistently.

I don't think anyone stopped to think I might get tired or feel off colour, my job was to be employed from the beginning of the day to the end. It was my good luck that I liked, not hated, what I was doing and I did learn a number of skills.

I went to church regularly, attending nearly every Sunday the nearest church or preacher, Mr Sutcliffe always driving and Mrs Sutcliffe and I in our Sunday best. I was always the Fairbridge girl, Mrs Sutcliffe's help, and I can't remember anybody ever offering me the hand of friendship or companionship.

Verandah lattice work of the type Flo painted

Sketch by Mavis Hayes

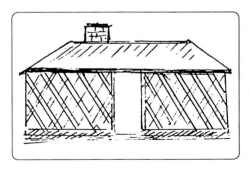

170

My stay in Damboring was to end abruptly and before twelve months were up.

One morning Mr Sutcliffe knocked on my door but, instead of staying outside, opened it, there was no lock, and as I turned over there he was in my very single bed beside me and had started to undress me and fondle my breast. I lay there stunned while completely innocent of what was going on, remember I had missed the lecture with Sister.

I had never asked questions of anyone, would not have known how or what to say, I hadn't a clue about sex, my bed was small and he was not and I was trapped where I was.

How far he would have gone or how desperate was his need, I'll never know for in a few moments all hell broke loose. Mrs Sutcliffe had luckily become suspicious of the quiet and silently came out to see what was happening. My door was burst open and there was her husband scrambling out of bed and myself minus my pyjama top. I remember that day as one long never ending vindictiveness.

Naturally I was to blame, she implied that I had opened the door and let him in, I would be sacked immediately and sent to Fairbridge on the first available train. I was to keep out of her sight, she didn't wish to see me ever again. I was to get Robbie's breakfast, speak to nobody and when not busy I was to shut myself in my room.

I was in a terrible state of shock, this high pitched anger and all directed at me. What had I really done, nothing. I hadn't gone into his bedroom, it was my bedroom that had been invaded. The shame, oh the blushing shame, it was my body that had been touched, never before had anyone touched my body. What could I tell Fairbridge, for she would tell them her own distorted story.

It was her pride that had been hurt and she would distort the rumour about me that someone had cruelly made up, now she was shouting that she always believed it was true. In the height of her hurt pride, she screamed anything she could think of at this girl whom they always imagined they had taken into their home and befriended.

Above the fireplace in the lounge room was a photo of their Rector, he was nicknamed 'Rats' by the congregation because of his initials, the Reverend Arthur T Sullivan. I didn't know then but I feel Mr Sutcliffe was very worried about his wife's reaction because somebody rang Rev Sullivan to come to the house.

It was soon after 10 am. Mrs Sutcliffe was lying down, prostrate in her bedroom. Mr Sutcliffe by this time must have been feeling as ill as I felt, no way could I put any food in my mouth, my whole body was a shuddering mass of shock. The atmosphere in the house was unbearable and all my fears of punishment were frightening the power out of my body.

When Rev Sullivan came, I was shut in my bedroom, everybody was keeping away from the house. Rev Sullivan spoke to Mrs Sutcliffe and then to Mr Sutcliffe and then he called me in, a tall man he was, and I was to discover fair and kindly. I wonder how I looked to him, the fear on my face must have been plain to see, and quietly he started to question me. Mr Sutcliffe was standing there too.

Rev Sullivan was trying to ask me had intercourse taken place. I hadn't a clue what he was trying to ask me because direct speech in those days didn't happen, and even if he had asked directly, I

172

wouldn't have known what he meant by intercourse anyway. He asked if Mr Sutcliffe had touched me and I, embarrassed, said yes but I couldn't bring myself to use the names of my body.

Your bottom was known as your BTM, your breasts as your chest, your belly as your tummy, so I could not say he fondled my breasts. Rev Sullivan sent me away to my room and went on talking to Mr Sutcliffe.

I was brought back time and again to be questioned gently by Rev Sullivan but could add nothing, understanding nothing. Did they know I was in a state of shock? Mrs Sutcliffe wanted only one thing, that I be punished for the affair, sacked immediately and sent back to Fairbridge. That there was no train until tomorrow was no concern of hers. I could sit on the railway station and wait, she wanted me out of the house.

Rev Sullivan offered to take me and put me on the train tomorrow and told Mrs Sutcliffe she was not to sack me but to inform Fairbridge that she had decided her health was better, that she no longer needed me. She was sending me home for my holidays and would be paying me holiday pay. He was to come back that night to collect me.

By now it was nearly 1 o'clock and a deathly silence was over the house. Automatically I had kept the kitchen fire going, the kettle boiling on the hob, for I had been sipping boiling water from a cup all the time, it was the only liquid I could hold in my shaking hands. Even my head and neck were shaking as I tried to sip the water and all day that is what I lived on. Mr Sutcliffe never spoke to me, I don't think he dared.

I never saw another soul that day. Heaven only knows how tongues were wagging, but in the course of the cross examination of Mr Sutcliffe with Rev Sullivan when I was there it came out that his wife was always fainting whenever he approached her. He said

173

she could just faint anywhere in the bedroom, but to me she showed no sign of illness, working herself and myself very hard. I think Rev Sullivan began to get the picture. Here was an attractive girl growing into womanhood and here was a frustrated man and therefore I had to go.

Everything about my departure remains a confused nightmare. I packed my bag, hid in my room till Rev Sullivan picked me up in his car. I don't even remember staying at his place till finally he took me to the train having bought my ticket and attended to all my needs. I don't even remember how I travelled and finally arrived at Fairbridge.

In the end I was welcomed back for my holidays. Luckily they were almost due as I had commenced work in August 1938 and it was now July 1939. If anybody in Authority had any doubts about my return, nobody asked and I was to tell one person only about my ordeal.

Cathy Watson, who was a good friend of mine, was also on holiday and we decided to go for a walk in the hills. It was a place of relaxation where we could feel at peace and talk. I had no intention of speaking about what had happened to me and the injustice of it all but, despite this, I knew I needed to tell someone, it was a secret too painful to retain.

I told Cathy the real truth for leaving and she told me the real truth of the small rabbit fur cape she had around her shoulders. She too was being used by the man of the house[21] but he would reward her with gifts such as the cape. I asked her how come it was never found out and she said he was always very careful, usually approaching her when his wife went away. Cathy had already been working there for two years and was going back.

---

[21] Tempe Woods wrote: "The girls are sometimes abused by outsiders who like to make such ignorant statements as 'All Fairbridge girls are immoral'."

174

She never fell pregnant so either he took precautions or was infertile.

Only two years ago I tried to track Cathy down but I was told she had committed suicide in the Swan River, which runs through Perth. Our lives were always so hellishly lonely. I feel sad but not surprised. God bless you, Cathy.

Flo (second right) and other residents outside the Girls' Friendly Society Lodge, Perth

51. BULLFINCH GOLD MINE

While I was back at Fairbridge after the ghastly affair at Sutcliffes' I learnt that Miss Missingham, the Teacher of Domestic Science at the Domestic Science Centre, had not yet been given a maid. She had seen me and we got chatting and I told her I would like to work at the farm school – it was somewhere I knew and I wanted to hide, I was afraid as well as embarrassed – and I would like to work at the Centre.

Faith Missingham realised the wisdom of this for she doubted if any outsider would care for the isolation of Fairbridge. It was different for teachers. They kept together, and besides they had cars and were able to escape.

She had me fill in an application form and wrote a covering letter. Fairbridge had not been so sure and until the final decision was made they could not have me idly standing by, possibly for three weeks or more. I was therefore sent to Bullfinch, a gold mine, to work with the Kellys, the manager and his wife.

What a trip it was from Perth, more than two hundred miles eastwards on the Kalgoorlie train. I guess I was travelling third class or perhaps second, but it wasn't first class. We did not even have that small task of buying our own ticket. The train seats were hard, oh so very hard, and I sat on this seat for hours. I can't recall anyone else sharing my compartment as I travelled all that way.

One of the first things I observed was miles and miles of flat ground covered with the most beautiful carpet of coloured flowers, everlastings. What a wonderful sight it was as I gazed at the scene I had never before witnessed. I was to actually walk among them

176

later, touching their heads, which already felt like dried pressed flowers. No wonder they called them everlastings for when picked and placed in a vase that is exactly as they stayed, never losing their crispness or colour. Western Australia is full of the most beautiful wild flowers.

I was met at the station and driven out to the mine and the manager's house. I felt immediately at ease with both Mr and Mrs Kelly. They were down to earth everyday people and very kindly.[22]

It was a small house, just as she had described it to Fairbridge in her application. The first thing that stood out to me was the screen door because buzzing all around were the largest blowflies I had ever seen. Ugh, I thought, and I said to Mrs Kelly: "I've never seen blowflies so big." She laughingly replied that they grew a special breed out there.

The other impact was the sound of the mine which worked round the clock, stopped only by breakdowns. For the first few nights it kept me awake. Yet after those first nights, or maybe a week, if the mine stopped during the night the silence was so stunning as to wake me up and not letting me drift off again till it resumed.

Tennis was played by the mine workers and by the wives of those who were married. Mrs Kelly encouraged me to take time off and play too. My life became so much easier and relaxed with them. I remember while playing tennis yelling out over the noise of the mine, Love one or Love fifteen or Deuce, whatever the case may be, and then halfway through this mighty yell the mine suddenly stopped, went silent and there was my voice yelling out like a giant's on the now eerie quiet.

Mrs Kelly did not work me hard, I never arose until 6.30 am. It was

---

[22] Geoffrey Thomas said: "There are so many good homes and good employers in Western Australia that it is really amazing that some of the children should be sent to rough, unsatisfactory places."

the first time I had the luxury of such late rising and I loved it. I cleaned this house, which needed it from all the dust floating around. I did all the normal household chores but no longer with any feeling of pressure. Work wasn't found for me when I had finished, my time was my own until required to prepare meals. I almost felt I was on holiday.

Mr Kelly called me one day into his office, Mrs Kelly was already sitting there. He asked me if I would like to go down the mine. I said: "Well, I don't really know whether I am brave enough."

He took me across to have a look, showed me the long black hole down which the mine shaft dropped. The fellows standing round grinned encouragement but somehow that dark hole was not yet for me. "Later," I said, "when I can pluck up more courage."

The men chuckled at me as they stepped into the lift and took off down the mine. I went back into the office with Mr Kelly and then quite casually he said to me: "Florrie, pick up that small enamel dish and give it to me, that one there with a bit of muddy dam water in it."

"Yes," I said as I turned to get it. First I tried to lift it with one hand and then, hearing a chuckle of laughter behind me, tried with both hands. Small that enamel bowl was but it was full of liquid gold and impossible for me to lift. He had enjoyed playing the trick on me and I too had enjoyed it.

Yes, I would have been very happy with these people, they would have shown me a humorous way of living, given me kindness and encouraged me to relax, and laugh again, to be perhaps the child I had never been, but it was too late.

I had grown past life that did not extract from me a challenge. I was seeking what? I did not know, trying to find a way to stretch my intelligence and didn't know how, but I did know I wanted the challenge of working in the Domestic Science Centre at Fairbridge. When Miss Missingham wired me to say the job was mine, to come as soon as possible, I was truly pleased but also I was loath to leave Mrs Kelly without help as she had been so good to me. I wrote to Fairbridge and told them it was a good job for someone who wanted to work easily without pressure.

Mr and Mrs Kelly, though not wanting me to go, also did not want to stand in the way of what they understood was progress for me. Sadly, yet excitedly, at the end of only three weeks I was returning to Fairbridge on those seats so hard, for that long train journey back. Mrs Kelly was sent another Fairbridge girl.

Flo and her first child Janice in
Canberra, where they were living

52. BACK AT FAIRBRIDGE, WORKING

The Domestic Science Centre had been financed by an English benefactor[23] from Cambridge, who would have been told about this need. The girls sent to the Centre were lucky, they would have the benefit of learning to cook, first aid, some millinery, as well as the normal cleaning and scrubbing.

Miss Missingham was an understanding person, somehow seeing in me the growing hunger to learn, somehow she understood. Firm as a teacher, very kind, she gave me responsibility right from the beginning.

My jobs were to be interesting and varied. I was the Maid, this was the title given by the State education department, which employed me, to the person holding my position. My wages were good but the responsibility of paying board was now mine.

Fairbridge gave me what was known as Staff quarters. Actually it was one of the boys' bungalows no longer in use and Miss Fain, a school teacher, and I lived here. I slept in the dormitory while she had what had been the Cottage Mother's quarters. I was content with the arrangement. Fairbridge was still keeping me under supervision as befitted my eighteen years of age.

Miss Fain and I got along very well. We dined in the Staff Dining Room, though I remember little about it or meals. My life was now wrapped up in the Domestic Science Centre. When I arrived at

---

[23] Lord de Saumarez. Ruby Fairbridge said it was in memory of his sister (Fairbridge Farm, p. 17). In The Farm School report, London said the £3,000 centre comprised a school, where girls aged 14 who had left the state school received technical training, and two cottages for older girls and trainees.

work, which was if I remember correctly 8 am, I would make percolated coffee for Miss Missingham. Oh that heavenly smell of good coffee and she would always say: "Have a cup too, Florence." Sometimes I did, sometimes I didn't. It was all so different from the ways I knew up till then.

Miss Missingham was tall and willowy, with a cultured speaking voice and very gentle manner, no cross words here only encouragement,[24] a lady. It was the sort of life and she was the type of person Miss Kittell had always wanted me to meet, though then I did not understand this.

Fairbridge had laid down only one rule, now that I was working as Staff my relationship with Fairbridge children was off limits except in the course of my duties. It was considered wrong, heaven alone knows why.

That did not apply to Fairbridgians returning for holidays. I was still free to visit the Club House any time. After all there was no other entertainment, but neither did I seek it. To talk, to laugh, to play and sing around the pianola, to dance together, to be ourselves, as far as supervision permitted, was all we asked. I was now happy and contented.

Part of my duties was cleaning Miss Missingham's flat which did not take up a lot of time. Washing and ironing were all part of my work too but my main duties were the requirements of the Centre.

I had to see that everything needed for the day's demonstrations was there, the meat, the vegetables, flour for whatever was being taught, and if my duties were up to date I was called in to share the lesson with the students. Before too long Miss Missingham was asking me to give the lesson, to write on the blackboard myself while she stood back and watched.

---

[24] Geoffrey Thomas said: "Miss Missingham is probably one of the best and truest friends that the Farm school children have ever had."

I remember the first time she asked me, the joy and the fear intermingled. Later only the joy remained.

We didn't have a good meat chopper and Miss Missingham ordered one from State Government stores, after all we did not buy our chops divided up and had to learn how to do these things ourselves. She sent me one day to collect the parcel from the store and when I brought it back and unwrapped it, there printed in large words on the meat chopper was 'I am British and of good temper'.

I took this motto as my own, not realising then it meant tempered steel. Australia was a land to which I had been transported and I had been kept shut away in an English speaking community, surrounded by newly arrived British children.

My contact through work with Australians had revealed no love for 'pommies' and only because my speaking voice gave me away did I admit my English birth. There was no shame in this, but you don't deliberately offer yourself up to be hurt.

So we kept to ourselves, always talking of home and one day going back, talking of the relatives we had left behind, those we could remember and wondering, as I always did: "Where is my brother Joe?" But no one was there to answer.

My days working at the Centre were full and fruitful and, though I was responsible for cleaning the whole Centre, the students as part of training had to scrub the top of their work table a sparkling white and sweep the floor around their table.

My duty was to resweep and mop, to touch up any table that needed it, but in particular to keep Miss Missingham's table snow white and its drawers filled with clean cooking appliances, to have the blackboards always clean and fresh chalk waiting and, during the school holidays, to clean the windows, cupboards and all the other jobs that were done then.

Miss Missingham had a car and took herself away, and I was trusted to do my work in her absence.

Much was changing. Germany had gone to war and our Fairbridge boys were joining up. I was now living in a different cottage, I feel it was Belfast Cottage near the corner store and Club House.

Canon Watson was now Acting Principal,[25] no Principal ever stayed the distance like Colonel Heath (he left in 1936). I liked Canon Watson. I was settled in my job but, living in my own space, little did I realise that children were no longer arriving at the farm school[26] because of the danger of bombing of the ships. It was said that a shipload of children had been bombed even though the ship carried the red cross symbol.

---

[25] In a report headed History of the debate between London and Perth, London said Canon Watson was the only Principal whom Perth Chairman Mr Joyner would tolerate as his appointment meant that 'the direction of the Farm School and After-care passed entirely to the Chairman'.
[26] In 1943, Tempe Woods wrote, only 29 school age children remained.

53. ENGAGED – AND DISENGAGED

In 1940 I became engaged to Fred Galloway. Fred was a good looking Fairbridge boy but I doubt if I would ever have become engaged to him except for Canon Watson. After all we were only walking out together, choosing each other's company in preference to going with the mob, strolling through the bush, sitting down holding hands, talking, talking and talking. It was a friend I really wanted, a friend to talk to.

One beautiful day we were sitting in the bush, basking in the sultry day, and then I lay flat on my back, hands held high above my head. Fred said: "Florrie, never lie like that in front of a fellow, you'll be at his mercy. He'll only have to grab your hands," and he demonstrated, "and you'll be unable to move."

He let go of my hands and I hurriedly sat up, blushing. I was still so shockingly ignorant. I did not comprehend fully what he was talking about, only how it must be to do with being pregnant or 'getting into trouble'.

Even with the girls I never discussed the 'facts of life'. Never realising the danger of my ignorance, I had the belief that as long as I kept my hand across my body whenever I was kissed, no boy could get close enough to make me pregnant. Though I was kissed I held my body well away, never permitting the boy to hold me close.

Canon Watson must have observed that Fred, who was now in the Army, and I were frequently alone. One day he called us to the Rectory to talk to us and, in his own way, talked us into becoming engaged. Fred told him he had no money for an engagement ring so, unbeknown to anyone on the farm school, Canon Watson bought him the ring to give to me. Of course I was excited, here I was engaged, not a real idea in the world what it was all about or what the future meant.

I stayed on working at Fairbridge and Fred went off to the Army camp. Although we were only engaged, Fred had his deferred pay made over to me and I promised to bank it in a separate account for him when he returned. Fred came back on leave just before his departure to the war zone. I was so excited to see him all dressed up in his khaki uniform, swaggering walk and all.

I said: "Fred, what are we going to do today?"

He replied: "Well, Flo, I'm going to the races, do you want to come too?"

I said: "No, Fred, I don't want to spend the day at the races."

He said: "You stay here then, I'm off, see you when I get back."

Though he did not know it, and though I did not break off my engagement on account of Canon Watson, that was the end of Fred. Anybody who on his last day with me could put going to the races first was not meant for me.

Unfortunately, Fred was to be a prisoner of war and when I did finally marry, I returned all his deferred pay to Fairbridge to be put into his Trust Account, and I really felt quite bad about it all.

54. I BLEW OUT EVERY LIGHT IN THE PLACE

I can't remember whether Miss Fain, the school teacher who I shared a bungalow with, had moved with me to Belfast Cottage, but I recall a couple of other people were there, Miss Fryer-Smith, Domestic Science Teacher, and Mrs Clarke, school teacher, and I remember how I nearly caused myself to have a nasty accident.

I used to do something I had been taught never to do, that is to plug in electrical equipment without turning off the power. To iron we would plug the electric iron into the electric light socket. Perfectly safe provided the light was off. I had got away with the bad habit of not switching off the power for so long that I never thought about it.

I placed a blanket underneath a cotton cloth on the table for ironing, then stepped on the chair, removed the bulb and with the iron plug in my hand started to push it into the light. Bang went everything in a loud explosion and I blew out every light in the farm school, frightening myself half to death.

I had black soot marks over the back of my hand and it took our Engineer, John Hickson, some time to find where the trouble had started and who was the culprit. He eventually arrived at Belfast Cottage, and I felt very stupid and sheepish as he lectured me nicely on what I already knew, the stupidity of my action.

I knew John then only slightly, having seen him in the Staff Dining Room for meals. He had taken over from John Young, a married man who had left to join up in the Air Force. John Hickson, still being unattached, was eyed off (looked at) by all the older girls but he didn't then take much notice of any of us. Two years later at the age of twenty one I was to marry John but at that time I was only nineteen and still had to ask permission for everything I wanted to do, which I always hated.

Around this time, I decided I needed to buy a bicycle to get myself around. Looking through the local catalogue, I ordered one to be paid for C.O.D. as it was known, or cash on delivery. It was costing me £7, which was a great deal of money in those days and was a lot for me to save.

I was paid £2 10s a week and out of that £1 4s for my board and 13s for my Trust Account were taken before I got my money. So I was left with 13s for all my personal expenses, writing materials, toiletries, etc.

The bike duly arrived at Pinjarra railway station and I was informed of its arrival. Too impatient to wait for the Fairbridge bus to pick it up next day I walked that evening into Pinjarra to collect it, paid for it, then found I couldn't unwrap it because it was so well wrapped for protection in transit. I finished up pushing it all the way back to Fairbridge, not one scrap tired, so thrilled to own my own bike.

It was called an XL and excel it did till finally many years later, while attending choir practice of all things in Orange, New South Wales, I had it stolen, never to be returned.

My bike had been a real asset because I had decided to learn the piano to again satisfy my love for music and I used to bike once a week to the Convent in Pinjarra for tuition by the Nun. She was sometimes impatient – nuns were known in those days as very sharp and abrupt – but also helpful. I could not always stretch an octave, having very small hands to suit the rest of me, and she worked out how we could overcome this.

Fairbridge had a piano in the Dining Hall and when I was off duty I would lose myself for hours practising, often having to be reminded

187

that meal times were on. Practice was no effort, I loved it all but alas, once I left Fairbridge, I had no longer the use of a piano and never could afford to buy one. Although I kept all my music books, I was never able to develop this love again.

Frank Parry, our farm school bus driver, was a good looking single man and we senior girls would gather around him giggling away, vying for his attention, and there was a time when I was his favourite. I liked talking to Frank, it was different from the Fairbridge chatter of the boys who were still at the show off stage of their manhood.

Not that I worked it out that way in those days, but Frank was mature, a man against their boyhood. Although in our naivety we could have been easily seduced, never did Frank in any way take advantage. I would be aware of a sweet excitement when I was with him, in expectation of I knew not what.

During this time at Fairbridge and because the war was on, it was decided that some of us would take First Aid and Home Nursing courses in Pinjarra. I still have my hard earned medallion. Frank drove the Fairbridge bus once a week to the lectures at the hospital.

One evening coming home the bus broke down. We all piled out knowing there was only one way to go, to push the wretched thing. As we did everybody started talking about the humorous things that happened at the lectures and we started saying silly things like: "What's your funny bone everybody?" and all yelling as we pushed: "The humorous," and practically dissolving on the road.

Finally exams were over and we had all passed. The Doctor who had put us through our training was called up and we all went back to Pinjarra to farewell him. That night he told us about doing his rounds and just how difficult it was to know how ill was this female patient, who would carefully attend to her make up each day

188

before his rounds. One day she hadn't had time and he found himself singing: "Oh the old grey mare she ain't what she used to be."

Suddenly a quiet dropped as he said farewell to his friends, and his hospital, and the tears coursed down his cheeks. It was a sobering moment. Frank Parry left to join up after that and the last I heard of him was that he was very ill with pneumonia. I never heard any more.

I made some good friends with Fairbridgians back on holidays, although more and more were joining up. John was becoming more and more involved in my life, although I did not plan it this way. Miss Kittell and Fairbridge encouraged us to marry away from the farm school friends we knew. The farm school said that to marry someone who was not Fairbridge gave us a family.

Looking back now it was the wrong advice, for only a Fairbridgian understood a Fairbridgian as we grew older. Our fierce independence, our hang ups, our need to know our beginnings, our parents, our family, where were they, why couldn't we be told about all we had left behind. That tremendous intolerance that lots of us developed because of the uncaring attitude and injustice of the whole system, and that awful inferiority complex, these would for ever influence our lives.

What did we know of normal marriage and normal home life when we had never experienced it? I never understood that normality was also the difference of opinion, the normal rowing and irritations of human relationships. Why, we hadn't even learnt to think independently for ourselves, we had never been allowed to make our own choices and our own mistakes. At twenty one years of age we were thrown into a world and a life for which we were ill prepared. Understandably many failed.

Towards the end of my time at Fairbridge, John, having his own car, drove to Mandurah for his day off. It was a Saturday or Sunday because I was free too, but not all day, so I said I would bike the sixteen miles to Mandurah and meet him there and I did.

What a glorious bike ride that was. I sang to myself as I cycled along and to my surprise John met me as he was returning, so we put my bike on the Essex and away back to Fairbridge we went. I never did see the sea that day.

All so innocent, carefree and happy. Then John joined up in the Air Force and was posted to Pearce in Western Australia.

A presentation at Sydney to launch a booklet, advising pensioners on housing, which had been produced by the Tuross Head branch of the Combined Pensioners' Association. Flo (second right) was branch president

My job at Fairbridge was coming to a close because my friend Miss Missingham had been given a transfer to Perth Domestic Science Centre.[27]

She thought it would be good experience for me if I put in for a transfer too. It was a big modern Centre and the move to Perth would also widen my horizons. She helped me by writing to the Principal of the Perth Centre and by talking to Canon Watson. Finally on 24 June 1941, at twenty years of age, I am employed at the Domestic Science Centre, Perth.

Work here was on a far larger scale than at Fairbridge, each floor containing different teachers for different subjects. I also had a special uniform to wear and had to ask permission of Fairbridge to buy it. My work for Miss Missingham was the same. I still went out to do all of the shopping for her lessons, to see that there was enough flour, sugar etc. My wages were still the same, and my board and what went into my Trust Account.

One of the funniest things I remember occurred when I had to go and buy brandy for cooking the Christmas cake. I had never been inside a hotel and here I was being told to go across to the hotel and buy a small flask of brandy.

I walked into the first hotel I saw, not to the bottle department because I never knew such a thing existed, no, straight into the men's bar I strolled. Dressed in my uniform, I was eyed off by the

---

[27] In The Farm School report, London said that Miss Missingham 'found herself thwarted' at Pinjarra and eventually became 'unequal to the contest' and left. Canon Watson then forbade her to visit the farm school.

men sitting at stools at the bar, grinning from ear to ear. No women were allowed to drink in the public bar which was the men's domain. They could go in there in their dirty work clothes and they were proud of being able to swear and carry on in a way they would not do in front of women.

I went up to the bartender, I can still see him looking at me with an amused smile. "Yes, miss," he said.

"Can I have a flask of brandy?" Not a muscle moved on his face. "What size?"

I wondered, what sizes are there. I replied: "I only want it for cooking a fruit cake for Christmas." I could feel the relaxed amusement. "Oh," he said. "In that case you'll only be wanting a small flask."

He reached for the bottle, put it inside a brown bag and away I walked, out of the bar, strangely disquieted but with no feeling of danger, then back to Miss Missingham and her lesson.

Later that evening when I was relating this to the girls at the G.F.S. Lodge where I was staying (the Girls' Friendly Society was an Anglican Church group), amid peals of laughter they told me about something called a bottle department. Then somebody told me I could have been mistaken for a prostitute.

"A prostitute," I said. "What's that?"

I can see the senior girl to whom we all turned looking at me and saying: "Oh, Florrie, we will explain that another time." Maybe if I had stayed at the Lodge long enough I could have learnt the 'facts of life' but the war was to change all that, all of us gradually going in different directions.

56. HUSH HUSH VISIT TO THE FORTUNE TELLER

Before I went to Perth I had this restless urge to study, to learn anything that would get me out of the humdrum work of the domestic. I had been taking a correspondence course in Nursing.[28] I had always loved physiology, the names of bones and parts of the body held for me a real fascination.

My drawings of bones and heart etc were pathetic and I would receive caustic comments with squiggles and query signs all over the page. I would blush as I read these comments but still went on, I really wanted to master the subject.

I carried on with the course for a while until somebody realised I was now working in Perth. I was then informed I would have to attend the Technical College instead.

Maybe arrangements could have been made but I was too unsure of myself to find my way to the College at night and I expected that if I asked Fairbridge they would say: "No," and I did not have the confidence to ask for help from the teacher or the others who would be attending the same classes.

Fairbridge did not know that I had been doing the correspondence course, it was good sometimes to do something no one knew about! I was also informed when I did see someone in Authority at the hospital at Perth that I was too small to be a nurse and would never be accepted. One look at me and they could not visualise me ever lifting a patient. My studies came to an end.

---

[28] Geoffrey Thomas said: "As for helping in a financial way any boy on to a Farm etc. or any girl to defray expenses for taking up Correspondence Courses in Nursing or anything like that, not once did I hear the matter suggested."

Once I was walking home from work when a car with three boys in it kept stopping beside me or pulled up in front of me, they were singing out: "Need a lift? Come on, we will give you a lift," and I very politely kept saying: "No, thank you, I want to walk."

I was beginning to feel decidedly frightened and was relieved when they decided they had had enough and drove away. Later that evening I relayed this to the girls in the Lodge, who told me to ignore it if it happened again and not to talk at all but just keep walking. I was very nervous for a long time after that but it never happened again.

The Lodge was a big boarding house with strict rules and if you broke these you were out. Fairbridge put me there when I went to work in Perth. We got breakfast and an evening meal. The girls at the Lodge came from everywhere, country, city, and were of all ages, all shapes and sizes, different religious denominations, and they worked all over Perth. They were very good to me, sensing that I was different from them all.

Marg, older than us all by a few years, was the one we all turned to for advice. Any sort of problem she seemed to have an answer for. We were all innocent teenagers or a little older, while she was late twenties or, looking back, even older.

One evening a serious debate took place, everyone feeling so sad as Jane, a very young pretty girl, sat sobbing out her news to Marg that she was pregnant. "Oh, what will I do?" she cried.

Marg replied: "Leave it to me, I know Bob (the person responsible), I'll speak to him."

A few nights later she was telling us all that Bob said he wouldn't marry Jane, he had proved his manhood and was puffed up with this fact, and was rearing to go and see who else he could trap. Poor Jane. I never did know the outcome but those words of Bob's rang in my ears. Proved his manhood. I didn't know him but I hated him.

Every Sunday morning at the Lodge breakfast was served in bed, mainly so that the Staff had a fairly easy day and somehow to convey to us a sense of Sunday being different. This breakfast consisted of hot buttered toast with tea served on a tray. Unfortunately, by the time we got the toast it was a cold soggy mass. You bit into it, the butter oozed out all down your face, but it was eat it or go without.

The rest of the day was free, except we were expected to attend church at least once. Often a group of us would catch the train and go to the Perth National Park, a very large flora and fauna reserve. They were great train rides and we always enjoyed ourselves wherever we went, arriving back tired and ready for a good night's sleep and another day's work.

The girls at the Lodge introduced me to a fortune teller, illegal then, it always had to be done hush hush. The girls had told me about a certain lady who told your fortune, how to get there by bus, her address, and away I went. I arrived at her street and wondered which house. I was looking up and down when a door opened across the road and a voice sang out: "Looking for me, dear?"

Realising this must be her, over I went, quite scared really. Nothing she told me that day ever came true, yet she was to prove a help to me. She said: "Florrie, I am going to burn a candle for you. No, I don't want any money." You always had to pay for the candle.

She said: "I want you to take great care when you are walking along the street, you daydream so much you are crossing the roads without knowing. Now when you leave here take care and stop daydreaming."

She was absolutely right, I had often gone from work to the Lodge without remembering crossing one of the many side streets. After her talk I started to make myself conscious of what I was doing.

I had really gone to her hoping to hear about happiness coming into my life. To hear that I would return to England and see my sister and brother, but nothing like that was foretold. The emptiness and loneliness were to remain. Daydreaming would continue to take its place.

Work went along well. The building I worked in, with its up to date equipment, fascinated me. I wanted to learn, and learn and learn. I hated being what now was classified by the Union as a cleaner. Miss Missingham's Assistant had at least some semblance of dignity, but a cleaner in those days, especially a female, was perceived to be a real drudge.

One day at the Centre I nearly blew myself up lighting the gas copper, nobody had explained that I should light the wand first, then turn on the gas, then apply the wand to the burner. No, instead I turned on the gas, took time lighting the wand, applied same to gas and sent out this mighty explosion. Someone came running but, apart from singed hair and eyebrows, I got off very lightly. At least the copper was lit.

I was in disarray, trying to gather my wits together, when this large rough bully of a man appeared. "Miss Brown," he said, at the same time grabbing my arm in a grip that hurt me, "I have come for your Union fees."

"What Union?" I said, as I told him to leave go of my arm as he was hurting me, I wasn't Fairbridge for nothing and I wasn't being pushed around by the likes of him.

"Cleaners' Union," he replied. I answered him: "I am not a cleaner, I'm Assistant to the Teacher." He said: "No Union there, we're taking you into the Cleaners' Union."

196

I hated his whole bullying attitude and answered: "Sorry, but I'll have to get in touch with the Principal of Fairbridge to see if I'm allowed to join, I can't do anything without their permission." It was the best stalling tactic I could think of on the spur of the moment, and he very rudely replied: "If you don't join Miss Brown, we will see you don't have a job."

I did of course join, but I would never pay my fees to him. Instead I used to walk to the Trades Hall, stroll into the office and pay. When I entered I used to hear them say: "Here comes Miss Brown." They knew my reasons for doing what I did. I was to learn later that all Union officials were not like this, but these bullying horrors turned so many people against them.

A recognition of the contribution which Flo makes to the community as a voluntary worker

EUROBODALLA COUNCIL
SENIOR CITIZENS AWARD

Mrs Florence Hickson

SENIOR CITIZEN OF THE YEAR

1986

C P VARDON
MAYOR
Council of Eurobodalla

John was training as a fitter armourer at Pearce. His father was the Chief Engineer of Perth in charge of the reservoirs. His parents and family – he had two brothers and five sisters – lived in the King's Park area, a lovely old home in beautiful rambling grounds, having its own tennis court. It was the sort of social background Miss Kittell would have approved of.

John's family, knowing of my background, were not sure I was the right person to marry their son. "Who was your Mother? Who was your Father?" and I took a mischievous delight in saying: "I don't know," without any further information. I continued to call in for meals, with or without John, as he had made this a stipulation while he was unable to get leave from the Air Force.

He decided he would teach me to drive, something I had been longing to learn. He still had his Essex car and, because I was so small my legs did not reach any of the pedals, he oxywelded a length on each pedal. I often wondered how he managed when he got in with his normal length legs.

But like so many beginnings in my life this too was to end before many lessons had been completed because John was posted away from Perth. For years afterwards, because I never did get to learn to drive until I was in my forties, I used to have nightmares about driving a car. I would start it and get going, but never could accelerate. I wasn't to lose this dream until I learnt to drive.

John was posted to Point Cook in Victoria and I was left to correspond with him and with visits to King's Park and enjoying meals with his family. I thought: "Why not join the Forces too?" I went along to join the Army. They were taking women now. I got the form to fill in and where it said what occupation I filled in cook. Next I had to write to Fairbridge for permission, which was agreed, but before I heard any reply back from the Army I turned twenty one.

Now no longer bound to ask for permission, the step that I would not take so that I could marry John earlier, I was finally free to do as I pleased. John asked me to go to Victoria to be married and I agreed, for there was no way I could return to England because of the war.

I was lucky enough to catch the last train that civilians were allowed to travel on and that was after filling in numerous papers answering so many questions. To be married was not really a good enough reason in the eyes of the Authorities who wanted to keep all trains for troop movements.

I arrived in Melbourne knowing no one at all but John had friends of his family, the Baldwins, in one of the city's suburbs, Kew, and I was to go there. I bought my wedding dress that day and had my hair set for the great occasion.

Everyone was so kind when I told them I had just arrived from W.A. I walked around Melbourne till it was time to arrive at the Baldwins' place. I was so tired I lay down and went sound asleep for a couple of hours, much to their amazement. How could anybody go to sleep like that on their wedding day?

Alone but for these people who were so very good to me, I walked around to St Hilary's Church. Just five people to see me married but, when I came out, there stretching from the church door to the road was a long red carpet and lined up on either side a troop of Girl Guides.

Twelve months later John was posted to Goodenough Island, off

199

the coast of New Guinea, with the Americans and I was left to bring up our first child, Janice. I was now living in Canberra alone and very lost.

After the war we did not return to Western Australia and I gradually lost all contact with Fairbridge. I did return to England, in the 1970s, and met my sister again after more than forty years.

A few years later she got a copy of her birth certificate for pension purposes and found that she was a year older than she had always thought. Much more than that, however, she discovered the circumstances of her father's death and realised we were half sisters, not full sisters.

I did not return to Fairbridge until June 1987, to what I thought was going to be a joyful reunion with past farm school friends. Instead, as I walked into the Church of the Holy Innocents, the wall that was around my heart broke as the horror of so many children being deprived of home and family was brought home to me.

That so many could have lost all knowledge of their beginning, and that so few people were aware that it had happened, was beyond my understanding. My tears came then, and it took eighteen months of counselling to dry them up, coupled with the knowledge that, at long last, someone out there had found my brother, whom I had longed to find since I was five years of age.

It was 13 February 1991 when Margaret Humphreys, from the Child Migrants Trust in Nottingham who comes to Australia regularly to help those who were migrant children, interviewed me in Sydney. It was only three weeks later, back in England, that she found Joey.

It was May 1991 when I returned to England and was finally united with my brother.

I was married for eighteen years. One of those was heaven.

When Janice was five a psychiatrist told me to leave my husband. But because of Church teaching and because I felt that love must be given a try, I stayed on. In the end I was told by a psychologist that if I did not leave before I became ill I would end up in hospital and never come out. I left.

Janice was employed at Newcastle in New South Wales and my son Ian was at technical college. My other daughter Wendy came to live with me. I took myself to college to study shorthand and typing part time, I wanted a job that held some dignity. It took me eighteen months to reach an employable standard.

My first job was in an estate agent's office on the North Coast of N.S.W. It was then that I realised how green I still was. I was looked on as easy game. Luckily I was able to cope with it safely, but owing to pressure being put on me to bed down with clients or lose my job, I finally left. I was sorry, I liked the work.

I applied for and was given the job of secretary to the Rector of St Michael's Church, Wollongong, south of Sydney, after having been sent to the Bishop of Sydney to see that as I was divorced this did not act as a handicap to my employment. Divorce then was taboo. His words to me were: "I think you have suffered enough."

My next job was to take over the running of the newly organised Opportunity Shop where we sold second hand clothes and furniture to help the Home Mission Society fund its work on the South Coast. This shop did very well and I really enjoyed the work.

Nervous sensations that had begun to attack me grew stronger, showing up in a feeling of unreality, as if I floated between earth and heaven and was no longer breathing. I used often to stop and find my pulse to see if my heart was still pumping. At this time I was singing in the choir, it seemed to help with my breathing.

I was put in touch with a psychiatrist attached to the Anglican Cathedral in Sydney, whom I had seen years before, and I remember him saying: "Do you realise how you keep coming back to both Fairbridge and the Church?" I hadn't realised how they were still dominating my life.

He also said: "What is this outsize guilt complex you have got?" I realised I was carrying guilt over my divorce, remembering that the Church said this was a sin. He asked: "What do you think of divorce?" I replied: "I think in some cases it has to be." He agreed but said until I believed it I would never be cured.

These questions happened in sessions over months. One day he said: "Florence, how do you feel?" I replied: "I don't care whether I live or die." He said: "Florence, I am going to put you into hospital." I was in his hospital for a month. (I was lucky to have my job kept for me.) I was given shock treatment of insulin injection daily, it knocks you out. I was discharged at the end of the month and went back for my usual consultations.

My visits grew further and further apart until in the end he said: "Florence, I am saying what we never say in psychiatry, you are cured." I never had to go back and at last I began to understand I was not an inferior human being, though I did not realise that there was still a lot of hidden anger and sorrow and this was not revealed to me until I returned to Fairbridge in 1987.

I left the Opportunity Shop after injuring my back there and having to take eight weeks off on Union benefit. The specialist suggested I find a different job where I was not lifting heavy soft weights.

I got a job in a hotel as a cook. I loved cooking and built up the clientele. The pay was very low, the bar attendants receiving more than the cook so I decided to learn bar work. I had to join the Liquor Trades Union, where women were really only tolerated, it was very male dominated. I decided that as I had no choice about being a Union member I would attend the monthly meetings.

The result was that I was elected the first woman President on the South Coast. This was not a paying job, it meant only that I presided at all meetings.

I soon found I was on the receiving end of nasty gossip and it was impossible to hold a job for any length of time. I discovered that my employer would be rung up by the Union and told they had a Union stirrer working for them. Male Union officials found me a threat. So I started working for myself and I ran a snack bar in a club. I was very successful according to the accountant who prepared my tax return, but the Union started to hound me again.

An election was taking place for a new Union State President and I was working with others for a change at head office in Sydney. The old guard was defeated and some weeks later I got the job of secretary of the local office in Wollongong. I now belonged to the Clerks' Union.

Finally my back gave me too much pain and I retired on the ground of ill health aged fifty five. I sold my house in Wollongong which I was still paying off on a mortgage and this enabled me to buy land in N.S.W., first on the coast and then inland.

I have lived here for twenty years. There are twenty six acres, which Wendy and her husband Jeff farm, running cows and calves on the land. They live on one part of the property and I on another part. I built up the garden and vegetable patch, and grow all my own fruit such as figs and peaches. Wendy has two daughters, one still at High School.

Janice had two daughters, but one died of leukaemia. She also has a son. Janice works in a bank part time, her husband Bernie used to work for a large supermarket chain. My son Ian was a wool classer, then designed and built shearing sheds, and is now a licensed builder. His wife Lynette works in a bakery, plus lots of other jobs.

My sister Gwynneth was seventeen when she returned to Liverpool, where she and her husband Bill live. They have been married fifty seven years. Bill was in the Navy in the war and then worked on the docks for thirty six years. They have three children, a son aged fifty three who has a strawberry farm on Guernsey and twin daughters aged fifty, six grandchildren and five great grandchildren.

My brother Joe has lived in Warrington since 1963. He had a cobbler's shop in Wavertree but thought he could do more with his life and at the age of forty three became a student nurse. He qualified and was a charge nurse in a psychiatric hospital for twenty two years. His first wife Rose was still alive when I went to England in 1991. Now he is married to Marion and she brought with her five grandchildren. Joe says he has 'a smashing life now'.

Much of my time is spent doing voluntary work, particularly for the retired age group. I have worked in organisations that have fought for better conditions for pensioners and still are fighting.

I have felt compelled throughout my life to fight where I perceived injustices to be done.

HISTORICAL BACKGROUND TO FLO'S MIGRATION

The Kingsley Fairbridge Farm School at Pinjarra, Western Australia, which was 'home' to Flo between 1928 to 1941, received its first party of children in 1913. It still functions in connection with youth work.

Kingsley Fairbridge saw migration from a colonial standpoint. He was born in 1885, a fourth generation South African. His childhood reads like an adventure tale: unconstrained by school until he was eight, he then left at 11 and helped his father, a land surveyor, to chart Rhodesia (now Zimbabwe). At 13 he 'walked on the outskirts of the Empire'.[29]

He had a dream: to fill the empty lands of the Empire with farmers. The dream became more detailed when, as described in his Autobiography, he visited England in 1903 and saw the mass of people in cities such as London, the overcrowded, insanitary conditions in which many lived. In the East End he saw two women fighting as children watched and a man hitting his wife – which drew his comment (p. 130) that the 'negroid races are not supposed to hold women in respect, but such an incident as this I have never seen in Africa'.

However, he realised that it was no use transplanting adult city dwellers and expecting them to excel at rural skills. "Eight years' schooling would barely give a man a glimpse of the possibilities which lie before a farmer," he said (p. 131). Thereafter, his dream took shape as filling the lands with homeless and destitute children.

Instead of housing them in the orphanages and workhouses of

---

[29] The Autobiography of Kingsley Fairbridge; London, 1927, p. 40

Great Britain, they would go to farm schools in Greater Britain. "This will not be charity, it will be an imperial investment," was his contention (p. 174). Instead of having to take 'small' jobs at 12 or 14 for which they would be too old at 18, they would be trained for work that would last a lifetime as well as helping to build their colony.

He was one of 50 Rhodes Scholars at Oxford University who in 1909 formed what came to be known as the Child Emigration Society and in 1912 he and his recently married wife, Ruby, set out for Western Australia, whose Premier favoured farm schools.

Empire settlement
Two years before Kingsley Fairbridge died aged 39, a new phase in British migration was sanctioned: direct encouragement by Government, in the shape of grants and loans.

The policy was set out in the 1922 Empire Settlement Bill, the second reading of which was presented to the House of Commons by Leo Amery, later Secretary of State for Dominion Affairs. He was to write the preface to the posthumous publication in 1927 of Fairbridge's Autobiography.

Fairbridge's emphasis on farmers was echoed in the Bill and had been spelled out by the Dominions at a conference in 1921. They wanted to open up their lands. They also wanted women for household work; there was a shortage of women.

Amery played up the benefits of making farmers the key to the Empire's economic regeneration. The Dominions would provide the agricultural goods that Britain wanted and buy the manufactured goods that Britain produced. Britain would cut surplus population and unemployment queues, so saving on cash handouts, a continual 'weakness to the nation'. Another plus: the supply of men and resources for imperial defence in the event of another war.

Some MPs had reservations about certain aspects but none opposed the Bill as such. There were doubts about whether Britain could afford to lose its best people; about accentuating Empire trade at the expense of trade with the larger European market; about paying to settle people in the Dominions, breaking up families, when land in the Scottish Highlands could be brought into production rather than deer forests extended further.

Support was forthcoming for white settlers – Captain Gee said[30] that in Australia and Canada they would help 'to do away with the bogey of the yellow peril. . . . the Japanese peril', and for migration of the young – Sir Donald Maclean said (p. 604) that they were 'much more likely to make an efficient citizen in the Dominions, than those who have reached an age of 25 or 30 years'.

Other MPs believed that the British race was one people and whether they lived in Britain or the Dominions was immaterial, and that migration offered the best chance to get on, as well as being the way of putting British shipping right.

Tension between the UK and Western Australia
Tension was always a feature in the relationship between the Child Emigration or Fairbridge Society in the UK and the farm school and the Fairbridge Society in Perth. Ruby Fairbridge makes clear in her book[31] that the UK Society had no idea of the difficulties of starting and running a farm school thousands of miles away.

It held back on vital funding, it demonstrated bureaucratic mentality, it believed children should be 'managed'. After the first world war, for example, it sent out former members of the armed forces although obviously for a farm school 'one should turn to the Agricultural Colleges and the University Faculties of Agriculture when looking for the educated assistants so desperately needed' (p. 161). In 1915 the UK Society had wanted to close the farm

---

[30] Parliamentary Debates, Commons 1922, vol 153, p. 600
[31] Fairbridge Farm. The Building of a Farm School; Perth, WA, 1948

school but it kept going in the remaining war years largely because of Western Australian efforts, including the backing of the Perth Society. In 1919 the latter was incorporated by Kingsley Fairbridge, its resulting autonomy meaning it was outside UK control.

After Fairbridge died the tension heightened and 'disquieting reports' about children who had left the farm school for work reached the London Society by 1935, the year Flo had her first job. Some Old Fairbridgians were in a 'pitiable condition'. They had had no attention from Pinjarra and had drifted into squalor and disease.[32] Such reports would have been unwelcome; the year before, in 1934, London had opened a £100,000 appeal, backed by the Prince of Wales, to build three more farm schools modelled on Pinjarra.[33]

London could, of course, stop sending children and this it did after July 1939. Perhaps it was only coincidental that a couple of months later the second world war started and might be expected to cause a hiatus. Possibly it had something to do with Barnardo's decision not to send children to Pinjarra after 1939 because of general unease about them going to organisations where it lost control of their future.[34]

Although London had to provide maintenance money, it finally imposed a cash squeeze in 1943, telling Perth that its ultimate responsibility must be covered by ultimate control and that Perth must use reserves to pay for current expenses.[35]

London also went to the Dominions Office for help, reporting that of the four farm schools for which it was responsible (two in Australia and two in Canada) only Pinjarra was not managed

[32] Report headed History of the debate between London and Perth
[33] Special report, 1934, p. 31; Annual report,1934, inside front cover
[34] Select Committee into Child Migration, Western Australia Legislative Assembly, Interim Report November 1996, p. 12
[35] History of the debate between London and Perth

satisfactorily. Over the last seven years it had tried persuasion, including the 'infiltration of first rate staff', but to no avail. The Perth chairman Alfred Joyner and, to a lesser extent the secretary A F Stowe, were blamed, being in effect the operative part of the management committee.

The critics
Apart from after-care, such as checks on employment conditions, the other aspect of anxiety centred on how the children were being brought up. Miss Missingham, the understanding and encouraging teacher for whom Flo worked at the Domestic Science School, went in person to London in 1938 to appeal for a more enlightened direction of the farm school.

London's hand was forced to some extent by Geoffrey Thomas, an adult accompanying the July 1939 migrants. He had intended to buy a farm but, seeing the farm school was short-staffed, stayed to help. He arrived at London's office in February 1941, paying his own way back especially to urge root and branch reform of Pinjarra.

A summary about Thomas and his visit indicates that he delivered an ultimatum: either you do something or I will. He refused to believe what he had heard, that London would listen but was impotent to act. London was left in no doubt: "Our impression of this single-minded and entirely disinterested man is that if we failed to make an assault on the position, he would feel himself compelled to seek redress for the children elsewhere." Even so, it was getting on for three years later that London went to the Dominions Office.

Geoffrey Thomas was not against the farm school itself. Quite the contrary. He ended his report with the call: "With more vision, courage and vigour, care, sympathy and humanity, the Fairbridge, Pinjarra, scheme could be converted from what it is into one of the finest and most Christian, and soul-saving and Empire-building

209

movements of this or any time." As a supporter, his criticisms are all the more powerful.

Although Flo does not remember him, much of his report reflects what she tells, as does the report of another critic, Tempe Woods. Also from the UK, she took a party of children to Pinjarra in 1938 and was after-care officer for three years at the start of the '40s.

Highlighting the chasm between image and practice, as Thomas had also done, Woods was blunt that this was 'wrong'. No matter what the Fairbridge Charter published in England said, and on which the appeal for funds was based, Pinjarra staff were told that it was farm school policy to place the children only as agricultural labourers and domestic servants (as indeed was set out in 1922) and if training for any other work began the Government grant would stop. "The wastage of talent . . . is what distresses us most," Woods wrote in 1943 to the London secretary.

In a general policy statement London stressed that no bargain had ever been struck with Australian or Canadian Governments to supply farm labourers and domestic servants in return for a grant.

London knew, however, that even if talents lay in other directions there was little chance of an alternative to the stipulated occupations, at least until the children were 21 when, as Geoffrey Thomas pointed out, it was often too late to change course. In comments (above a 1945 letter) about a survey of available children, London said that Australia was to be partially industrialised, which should ease 'the hard demand' that child migrants went only into agriculture.

The farm school
The children knew that their occupational destiny was determined and, London said in its summary about Geoffrey Thomas's visit, 'as soon as they are old enough to think, they feel almost fatalistically that they have no escape from being a <u>depressed</u>

210

<u>class</u>'. After-care visits revealed their sense of hopelessness, of resignation, of being marooned.

Thomas said that one of the farm school's greatest ideas was to provide a proper home atmosphere. But the cottage mother was so busy with domestic chores that she had neither time nor energy to give children individual attention. New arrivals were split up indiscriminately, as were siblings. Friends were separated when they became seniors and moved to a different cottage. No one asked the children for their views. It was the antithesis of what was intended.

Geoffrey Thomas questioned disciplinary measures, often for trivial matters such as insubordination. One was to send children out to work early, another was to put them into Salvation Army Homes at Gosnells, WA, or houses of correction. London told the Dominions Office: "In 1942, one in seven of 'Pinjarra' children were in these homes."

The children, who received a standard state elementary education until they were 14 or so, were held back scholastically, London said. Those who studied in their own time with the unpaid help of their headmaster to get the Junior Certificate were refused permission to enter for the exam when the time came.

Cheap labour
Seniors who were supposed to be having training for a year or two, as well as trained children working at the farm school, were used as cheap labour. This is a recurring theme in child migration[36] and confronted the Fairbridges when they arrived in Western Australia.

Kingsley Fairbridge was invited to put his case to a Labour women's organisation which, said his wife, had 'heard that we were preparing to bring child slave labour into a country which

---

[36] Barry M Coldrey, 'A Thriving and Ugly Trade'. The First Phase of Child Migration, 1617-1757; Victoria, Australia, 1995, p. 1

prided itself on being the working man's paradise' (Fairbridge Farm, p. 56). His eloquence failed to reassure them that child migration did not mean a lowering of wages.

Nearly 30 years later Geoffrey Thomas was driven to describe the procedure for placing children in work as 'at times reminiscent of a cheap labour bureau'.

Their training showed how they were regarded. A boy who opted for engineering was placed with the engineer but after a few weeks removed for 'important work' such as running messages for the head matron and office staff, weeding and watering the Fairbridge House garden, and digging, cleaning and relaying drains.

Girls fared no better, especially at the Rectory, home of the acting principal Canon Watson, where their working day could last from 6.30 am to 8 pm. "These hours are too long altogether for growing girls," Thomas said. They were also expected to know what they were doing, quite at variance with the fact that they were there to be trained.

Would-be employers were rarely if ever vetted, despite the general policy statement pledge that the Society stood *in loco parentis* to the children and this, in general, meant that they should be under its watchful eye until they were 21. Usually the first the children got to know where they were going, said Geoffrey Thomas, was when they were leaving for the station and were handed an envelope with their ticket and their employer's name and address.

Little seemed changed since 1935. Inadequately supervised girls became pregnant, possibly ruining their lives. Children were sent to unsuitable districts: a boy with asthma should have gone to a comparatively dry area but was in a wet rainfall one. They had no guidance: an Old Fairbridgian sent for his trust account savings so that his employer could help him develop some land. What the debt-ridden employer wanted was the cash, which she took.

As for wages, London told the Dominions Office that trained children kept on at the farm school were unpaid. Those out at work received low pay. In 1939 a girl of 16 was looking after five small children in a family and doing the general work of the house for 12s 6d (52 1/2p) a week. One boy worked for three years without any holiday or increase in his pay of 15 shillings a week.[37]

Regarding Kingsley Fairbridge's dream to people empty Empire lands with farmers, in 1935 a London subscriber gave £5,000 to help Old Fairbridgians acquire smallholdings.[38] The money was also to help gifted and ambitious Fairbridgians qualify for work other than farm labouring or domestic service, London said in its summary about Geoffrey Thomas's visit. Eight years after being sent to Perth, it was for the most part unused.[39]

Eventually London was required to effect an overhaul[40] by the 1948 Children Act 'covering the care of children without family protection'.[41] This meant that London could no longer act as agent for sending cash and children but would have to retain sufficient powers over their care, training, placing and after-care 'to satisfy justice as well as the regulations'. It also meant that the Society was compelled to revise its relations with autonomous Fairbridge societies overseas.

London's relief at believing that it was finally bringing Pinjarra into line, with regard to post-war migrant policy, is palpable. That it did so is uncertain, Margaret Humphreys[42] noting the warning in 1948 by former Pinjarra principal Mr A D Paterson (1936-c. '37) that people associated with past practices were on new committees running the farm school.

– Anne Bott, Editor

---

[37] Report headed The Farm School
[38] History of the debate between London and Perth
[39] Report to the Dominions Office, 1943
[40] Fairbridge Farm Schools (Incorporated). Reorganisation plan
[41] Typed comments starting 'The Society will be required'
[42] Empty Cradles; London, 1995, p. 353

FAIRBRIDGE DOCUMENTS

The following documents in the Fairbridge Archive were used. If no date is given, the document was undated:

D296/H Emigration policy: Geoffrey Thomas report headed Confidential, Kingsley Fairbridge Farm School, Pinjarra; summary headed Mr Geoffrey Thomas; report June 1st 1943 headed Private and Confidential to the Secretary, London, from Tempe Woods; report noting As taken by Sir Charles Hambro and Sir Wm Campion to Lord Cranborne, Dominions Office, 26/11/1943; attached to the above a report headed The Farm School; report headed History of the debate between London and Perth; Kingsley Fairbridge Farm School, WA. Constitution of the Governing Body; letter April 2nd 1937 to Perth Chairman Mr Joyner from London Chairman L R Lumley; summary headed Survey of children likely to be available, above a 7th September 1945 note from Charles Hambro to Secretary of State for Dominion Affairs.

D296/C Policy, planning and finance including D296/C2 Policy documents such as the charter: typescript note, unsigned, starting 'Mr Buckley has sent the draft declaration'; letter 17th December 1945 to Gordon Green from Charles Hambro; summary headed Fairbridge Ideal; prospectus headed Fairbridge Farm Schools Inc., starting Object: The Object of the Society; document headed General Policy; Fairbridge Farm Schools (Incorporated). Reorganisation Plan; typed comments starting 'The Society will be required to subscribe to the new regulations'.

D296/C3 Minutes, Annual General Meetings 1925-29, 1933-38.
D296/D1 Annual reports 1923-1938.
D296/J2 Pinjarra: code of the school; maintenance agreement; general correspondence, letter from A F Stowe to Gordon Green 23 January 1940; church: plans, correspondence; cottages: plans, correspondence; register, Pinjarra.

Bill of Bulwell

by Bill Cross

This is the story of a Nottingham working man. As a child, Bill watched returned soldiers from the First World War live in poverty. He saw miners turned away from the pits each day after seeking work. He vowed he would never become a soldier or a miner. But he became both.

'Ordinary' Lives **1**

Series Editor: Ruth I. Johns

BILL OF BULWELL by Bill Cross is available through bookstores or Libraries. Or it can be ordered direct from Plowright Press, P O Box 66, Warwick CV34 4XE £6.95 (post free UK). ISBN 0 9516960 5 X

Alice
from Tooting (1879-1977)
by Alice Mullen (1879-1977)
Including recollections of her daughter Bertha Mullen (1910-)

Few working class women of Alice's generation wrote their life story. We share her endurance, beliefs, frail health, ambition to improve in her work, her parents' marriage break-up, two World Wars, being a mother and a stepmother, and a content old age living with her daughter in Chard.

'Ordinary' Lives ②

Edited by Anne Bott

ALICE FROM TOOTING by Alice Mullen (1879-1977), including recollections of her daughter Bertha Mullen (1910-). Available through bookstores or Libraries. Or it can be ordered direct from Plowright Press, P O Box 66, Warwick CV34 4XE £8.95 (post free UK). ISBN 0 9516960 4 1